whistlekick Martial Arts Radio Presents

LEGENDS OF THE MARTIAL ARTS

Jeremy Lesniak

wK Books

Contents

Introduction 7

Bill "Superfoot" Wallace 9

Sensei Fumio Demura 25

Don "The Dragon" Wilson 40

Grandmaster Cynthia Rothrock 89

Senior Master of the Arts Jeff Speakman 115

Grandmaster Jhoon Rhee 151

Legends of the Martial Arts

INTRODUCTION

In an instant, the power of the words in this book increased by an exponential magnitude.

On the day I am writing this, Sensei Fumio Demura passed away.

I do not want to write a somber introduction for you. I want to impress upon you the importance of appreciating the time we have together.

Along with Grandmaster Jhoon Rhee, this anthology now contains interviews with two groundbreaking martial artists whom we were fortunate to speak with while time allowed.

The stories told in this collection are impressive, motivational, heartwarming, inspirational, and even hilarious. As you will read, these legendary martial artists have set the bar high for those who came after them, folks like you and me.

How high can we push that bar in our time?

How will *we* inspire the martial artists of the future?

Jenni Nather

Director
Whistlekick Book Division

Bill "Superfoot" Wallace

"Bill Wallace is not only a legend but another great friend. Not only does Bill bring his martial arts expertise to the world but his infamous sense of humor."

— Cynthia Rothrock

"He's a really funny guy and always supportive."

— Fumio Demura

"I have had the pleasure to meet and be around Bill Wallace on many occasions. One must first be overtaken by his obvious sense of humor and wit. But you will quickly realize that these attributes come from a deep intellect that he will share with you in good time."

—Jeff Speakman

Interview was conducted on June 10, 2015.

Jeremy Lesniak: Hello everyone, and thanks for tuning in to Episode 14 of whistlekick Martial Arts Radio. I'm your host, Jeremy Lesniak, and I'm also the founder of whistlekick, makers of the best sparring gear on Earth, as well as apparel and accessories for traditional martial artists.

If you're new to the show, you can learn more about our products at whistlekick.com, and you can learn more about the podcast including all of our past episodes, show notes for this one, and a whole lot more over at whistlekickmartialartsradio.com. While you're there, don't forget to sign up for our newsletter, full of information about us, discounts, and useful martial arts content.

It's an honor to bring you this episode with Bill "Superfoot" Wallace. There are few in the martial arts that don't know of his amazing career, but after listening to this, you'll know all about him. Mr. Wallace speaks candidly about his entry into martial arts, his catastrophic injury, and even about the loss of some very good friends. Despite the seriousness of some of the topics, his trademark sense of humor is well on display. So, without any further delay …

Bill Wallace, welcome to whistlekick Martial Arts Radio.

Bill Wallace: Thank you very much, sir. I'm looking forward to it. I haven't done this for a long time, so I'm looking forward to working with you Jeremy. Thank you.

JL: Cool. Well, thank you for being here. It's quite the honor. So, everybody knows who you are. They know a lot about your history, but why don't you tell us why you got started in the martial arts?

BW: Well, I was a wrestler in high school and college, and when I joined the service, I went over to the main gym where I got into my permanent station to see if they had a wrestling team or anything like that. And the guy says, "Well, I don't know what it is, but there's a bunch of guys in white suits rolling around on the mats in the back." So, I walked in the back, and they were playing Judo. And that's how I got started playing Judo, because they didn't have a wrestling team, but they had a Judo team. And wrestling is very, very similar to Judo, so that's how I got started.

JL: What was it that you liked about Judo? Did you like it more than wrestling?

BW: Uh, no, no. It wasn't as much fun, because the rules were different. You could do this, you can't do that, you can't do this if you, when you throw people you can't grab the legs, and I went, "What the heck's this?" But then I learned to like it quite a bit, but wrestling is still my first love. But it was similar. You know, I did like the throws. I liked some of the take-downs. I liked the hold-downs. I liked the chokes. I liked the arm-bars. And I really enjoyed the throws.

JL: And of course, it was an injury in Judo that took you out of there and turned you into a kicker.

BW: Yep, it sure is. There was a guy who fell on my ... I tried to do a throw called ouchi gari, which is an inner reaping throw where you try to trip the leg, and a guy just collapsed and fell right on my knee and tore the medial collateral ligament.

JL: Now, were you into stretching and kinesiology at all at that point, or was it the injury that- ...?

BW: Not at all. No, that was when I was in the service. I went to college after the service. So, I had no idea about any of that stuff. I didn't ... The guy says, "Your knee's all screwed up. We want to operate," and I said, "What happens if you operate?" And he says, "Well, it might be okay, it might not be." I said, "What happens if you don't operate?" He said, "Well, it might be okay, it might not be." (laughs) I said, "You're not going to operate."

JL: (laughs) So, you didn't have the surgery?

BW: No, sir.

JL: Oh, wow.

BW: This was, this was back in 1966. There was no such thing as arthroscopic surgery. Back then it was called "exploratory."

JL: So, they would've had you all torn up?

BW: They would've, yeah. That would've … My career would've been done.

JL: Wow.

BW: I'd have been a spectator.

JL: So, there are a lot of stories that people have heard you tell, and you've certainly had a chance to meet and compete and train with a lot of the greats, but if you could pick just one story that you could tell us, I'd like you to share one. Your best martial arts story.

BW: Well, I guess the best martial arts story, in the competition aspect of it – other than, you know, training with my best friend, Joe Lewis, and several other people – is I was fighting a guy named Skipper Mullins in Dallas, Texas, 19- … 19- uh, God, 1972, I think it was. He was from Dallas, Texas. The tournament was at the U.S. Championships in Dallas, Texas. He was already National Champion, World Champion Lightweight, all this stuff. And a very, very good kicker, except he used the right leg. I used my left, he uses his right. And it was supposedly between Skipper and myself who was the best kicker. He won the Lightweight division, I won the Heavyweight division, if you can imagine me being a heavyweight.

JL: (laughs)

BW: But anyway, I won the Heavyweight division, and we're out there for the Grand Championship Match, and the head referee's a guy named Ed Daniels. The guy's 6'8", about 320 pounds. Chuck Norris was in one corner. Mike Stone was in the other corner. A guy named Pat Burleson was in one corner, and a guy named Jim Harrison was in the other corner. These are the absolute greats of point tournaments back in the 60's. And they were all really, really good friends with Skipper Mullins at the time. So, he called us to the center, Ed Daniels called us to the center, and he says, "Bill, look around," and I look around. I said, "Yes, sir." He says, "You see who the referees are, right?" I said, "Yes sir." He said, "You know what you're going to have to do to get a point, don't ya?" I said, "Huh?" He says, "You're going to have to nail him." I said, "What?" (laughs)

JL: (laughs)

BW: And back then, it was funny, you know, I could've touched him and been, "Hey, I could've killed him," but now, he said, "Now you got to." I said, "Oh, no." I said, "Really?" He says, "Oh, yeah." And then Skipper says, "Yep, Bill, to get the point, you're going to have to nail me." And I went, "Oh, great."

JL: (laughs)

BW: So, we bowed in. He came across the floor right off the bat and tried to sweep me, and I hit him in the chest with a hook kick and dropped him. And, you know, and no flags. And he's still on the ground. He's on the ground.

JL: (laughs)

BW: He stood up, and he says, "Good shot, Bill." And I said, "I didn't get the point." He says, "What?" And Chuck Norris says, "Hit him in the arm." Mike Stone, "Yeah, yeah, hit him in the arm, he didn't drop him, he hit him in the arm." And he opened up his gi top, and there's a big old red heel print right on his solar plexus.

JL: (laughs)

BW: And I said, "No matter what happens after that, Skipper, you and I are going to be the best friends in the whole world." And I went on and, you know, I dropped him with a side kick, and then I think I dropped him with a reverse punch after that, but we had a laugh, we had just an absolute ball. That was probably the best time I ever had in point tournament, when we did that fight.

JL: Wow, that's …

BW: And that was in 1972 I think it was.

JL: That's a cool story.

BW: Thank you.

JL: Even your beginning of your martial arts career was, you know, based around something that wasn't terribly positive, with the injury with your knee, but I'd like you to think about what your life might've been like without martial arts. And then of course, where you are, and how has the martial arts changed you, or made you a better person?

BW: Well, my father was raised to be a school teacher, so from day one, my father wanted me to be a school teacher, because he was a school teacher. And that's the reason I went to college, to be a school teacher. But then I started doing the martial arts and stuff like this so, everything just kind of ran in its place. I didn't want to teach school. I didn't mind working out and teaching Karate and stuff like that, but I never wanted to teach school. And you know, that was what was going to happen.

Then I started doing Karate. And he says, "When are you going to quit doing that stuff and get a good job?" And I said, "Dad, I like doing this." He says, "Well, you got to get a good job. Teach in a school." And then when I won the World Championship in 1974, all he did after that was introduce me as, "This is my son. He's a world champion Karate fighter." (laughs)

JL: (laughs)

BW: You know, I mean, ironically enough, it sounds funny, but I've never had a job. You know, this has always been my job, doing Karate, teaching Karate, competing. And it's always just been an absolute blast, you know. I mean here, I'm one of the few lucky people in the world that I get a chance to get paid to work out, and I get paid to have some fun, and work out, and get paid to do what I like to do.

JL: And you do it well, and you've been so inspiring to so many people.

BW: Well, thank you.

JL: On behalf of others and myself, thank you for doing that. And those are all …

BW: Oh, you're welcome, and hey, I've had a blast. I've had a blast.

JL: Those are all high points, but I'd like you to think about something on the other end of the spectrum, a low point maybe in your life that your martial arts training and experience and attitude was able to help you move through or overcome.

BW: Well, I mean, the low point of course, you know, very few of us that are competitors, that have trained a lot and are hard-core Karate people, have stayed married to our original wife. (laughs)

JL: Mm-hmm (affirmative).

BW: I mean, it's just because we're gone all the time, and no matter what happens, our wives are second. Martial arts has always been first for me, and everybody else, everything else, has been down on the list. It's kind of difficult to say, "Well, gee, you know, that's a really high point." Well, it's not. It sucks, as a matter of fact.

JL: Yeah.

BW: But the other low, you know, the other points that it helped me get through everything was, you know, I've had two really, really good friends of mine that have died because of drugs, you know, a guy named Elvis Presley, and a guy named John Belushi, and they both trained with me. They both worked out with me. And you kind of say, "Hey, you know, how can you look back on a crutch like that to have, when you can train, and work out, and beat the shit out of somebody, and go out and have fun afterwards, go out to have a beer, go out and have a Coke, go out and have a hamburger with each other without getting mad at each other?" But then, certain people need that added crutch, you might say. But that to me is a low point, because you're damned if you try to help somebody, and even they can't stop it themselves or they're weak enough that they have their friends tell them what to do. That was John's problem. John had too many friends that did drugs, and you can only say "no" so often, before you say, "Okay, I'll try it."

JL: Those are low points for sure, and there are a lot of people that have seen their friends go down that path.

BW: Oh, yeah.

JL: Been a little bit of time, but I'm sure the pain is still there for you, so I appreciate you being so open and sharing that with us. You've had a chance to train with, I mean, everybody. Anybody and everybody that you wanted to, and that's pretty cool, and something that most of us can't say, but who … If you had to pick somebody that was most influential throughout your martial arts career, who would that be?

BW: Joe Lewis. Joe Lewis. Simply because, the first time, because … Remember, I had a bad knee. I have a bad knee, my right leg, so I can't push off with it. What happens is, I started just like everybody else did in Karate. You take this Karate stance, and you try to … but I couldn't push off with it, because my knee was bad. And then I saw Joe Lewis compete. He was sideways. He turned totally, perfectly sideways, and worked that back fist, and a side kick. My first technique that I learned in Karate was a side kick, simply because I couldn't … I was in a cast at the time, so I couldn't move around, so the instructor, [Shimumoku], says to me, he says, "You do side kick. I show you side kick, and you do side kick."

He showed it to me, and I'm just standing there in the dojo, and it was closed, and I must have thrown 35,000 side kicks, not moving, just throwing them, just to practice the knee coming up and the side kick coming out to the side. Then I met Joe, which it was his number one weapon, the side kick. Then I began working out with Chuck, Chuck Norris, and people like that.

Probably another huge influence was a guy named Glenn Keeney, because when I went back to Ball State in Muncie, Indiana, I still worked out in Karate, but I didn't know any Karate schools around. Then I met a guy named Glenn Keeney at a workout, and we became friends. He was in Anderson, Indiana. I was in Muncie, which is about 18 miles away. Two or three times a week, I would drive over to his school and train at his school. We would spar, we would work out, beat the crap out of each other, and have an absolute blast. We did this for six years.

JL: Wow.

BW: We went on trips together, went on tournaments together. He talked me into going to tournaments with him, so we'd go to tournaments, and had a blast. Had an absolute blast.

JL: Competition obviously has been a huge part of your life. Maybe a bigger chunk of your martial arts career than anyone else.

BW: I would say 99% of it.

JL: Yeah. What was it about competition that kept you coming back? What did you love about it so much?

BW: It was fun. It was fun. You can actually go out there in the spar scene, and nobody wants to get hit in the face. Nobody wants to get hurt. In the competition aspect, the point tournaments, you can actually go out there and compete and spar. Even on the sides you could spar with somebody, and trust each other, and not get hurt. Sure, there's accidents that happen once in a while. There's some guys that are bullies, but for the most part, you go out there and spar, you can spar for an hour and a half, two hours, and not have any bruises at all, and that was the fun part of it. The fun part of competition was not the winning. It was just to spar around, having a blast. Having an absolute blast. I hate to lose by the way, but …

JL: (laughs)

BW: You know, the sparring was just, it was just fun. If you look at anybody, it was just fun. We never thought … I mean, Chuck Norris, his whole thing with sparring was, when he went to competitions is, it wasn't to win, it wasn't to do this. It was to get Karate students so he could have a nice, successful school.

JL: I've never heard that before.

BW: Yup, yup.

JL: What a riot. Was there anybody that you didn't get to train with that you would've liked to?

BW: Uh, I met Bruce Lee back in 1967. I would've liked to train with Bruce.

JL: What do you think you would've taken from that time with him?

BW: I have no idea. I have no idea. I imagine some of the movements. Some of the techniques involved and so forth and so on maybe. He used a lot of front hand and front leg techniques like I do, so maybe, maybe we would've melded somehow, an idea, because at that time in '72 … Well, I met him in '67, but in '72 just before he died, I was National Champion at the time, and he had seen me fight evidently, but I never did get to play with him, because at that time I was in Indiana, he was in California.

JL: That would've been cool. You may have-

BW: I would've liked that, yes.

JL: I was thinking maybe some of your footwork, because at the time it was so unique. Maybe you had some influence on Jeet Kune Do in there …

BW: Maybe, maybe.

JL: … that we don't even know about.

BW: Yeah, maybe.

JL: Do you have a favorite martial arts actor?

BW: Uh, yeah. Chuck Norris. Yeah.

JL: Why?

BW: It's only because I did a film. I did a film with him called A Force of One, and the most important part … He's one of a few guys that can do what he says. You know, he was a Karate person first, an actor second, but he became a decent actor, and genuinely a wonderful, wonderful, wonderful person. A great, great, great person. You can't do anything bad about that. One of my best friends in the whole world.

JL: Oh really? You guys are still …

BW: Yeah.

JL: … still close?

BW: Oh yeah. We still talk.

JL: Oh, that's great. You know, I think for those of us that grew up watching you guys, it's … we want to think that you're all friends …

BW: Yeah.

JL: … but to hear that you actually are …

BW: Well, we all, yeah, we all get along. We have something in common. It's one of those few times that we have something in common.

JL: What's your favorite martial arts movie?

BW: Uh … HA! A Force of One. No. (laughs)

JL: (laughs)

BW: I like them all. You know, if it's got some common sense into it, some good fight scenes. I like them all. I like to watch them.

JL: How about books? Any martial arts-related books that you'd recommend to people?

BW: I wrote three of them, and I liked all three of them. I have three books, "Dynamic Stretching and Kicking," "The Ultimate Kick," and "Karate Basic Concepts and Skills."

JL: Okay.

BW: Those are my three books.

JL: Well, we'll definitely have those linked in the show notes …

BW: Okay.

JL: … on our website at whistlekickmartialartsradio.com.

BW: Oh, good.

JL: You're still out there. You're still training and teaching, and I think that's awesome. What keeps you going? Are there goals that you're striving for here?

BW: I'm always … Well, I'm trying to keep … I'm going to try to keep myself in good shape.

JL: Mm-hmm (affirmative).

BW: Trying to keep my flexibility, trying to keep training, because it's fun kicking people in the head.

JL: (laughs)

BW: I really enjoy kicking people in the head. (laughs)

JL: Yeah. I mean that's … (laughs) ... How fun is that?

BW: Yeah.

JL: I've had a chance to watch you kick people in the head.

BW: That's right, and we shall do it pretty soon.

JL: That's right.

BW: In a couple months we will do it.

JL: Yup. This might be a good time to mention to folks, Sunday, August 16th-

BW: Yep. August 16th [2015], we will be there. We will be up in New Hampshire, or Vermont, excuse me.

JL: Vermont, yup. We'll have Mr. Wallace here in Vermont.

BW: Vermont, and having a blast. Yup.

JL: For one of his patented "Superfoot Seminars." What happens at those seminars, for people that haven't attended before?

BW: Well, we do a little bit of flexibility, explaining exactly how flexibility happens, why flexibility happens. The kicking techniques with the front leg that I use. The side kick, the roundhouse kick, and a hook kick. Different kinds … Different ways of using those kicks, ways of getting close enough to your opponent to throw those kicks. The speed involved in the kicks. The deception involved in the kicking techniques, and some of the boxing techniques that are used with the kicking techniques, and I put it all together at the end.

JL: It's fun.

BW: It is a ball. It's a … I have a blast. I do it, I've done it now for … I've done seminars now for 40-some years, and I still have a blast doing them.

JL: And it comes through. When I was fortunate enough to meet you and sit in on your seminar in Connecticut, it was clear that you were probably the one having the most fun …

BW: Oh, yeah.

JL: … in the whole room.

BW: Oh, I always have the most fun.

JL: It wasn't the students, and that says a lot for your passion to the arts and to teaching.

BW: Well, thank you.

JL: Just one more bit. Do you have any parting advice for people listening?

BW: Just have an absolute blast. Those people that are in the martial arts, there's different systems and different ways of doing something. There's different ways of kicking, different ways of punching, different philosophies, different ideas, and the most important thing is, have a blast. Have an absolute ball, because it's something that you can do absolutely forever, your entire life, and it's just fun, so do it.

JL: Very well said. Well, I thank you for your time.

BW: Well, thank you Jeremy. It was a pleasure, and …

JL: It's been a pleasure having you on here.

BW: … and the booties felt good this weekend. I wore the booties and they felt great.

JL: Oh. Well, cool. You okay with me leaving that part in?

BW: Sure, sure. Leave that part in, of course.

JL: Okay. All right. Well, folks, Mr. Wallace is talking about his whistlekick Sparring Boots that I gave him when I met him, and he put them on, and I got to watch him kick people in the head …

BW: Yup.

JL: … wearing them, and sounds like maybe some people took a couple shots while you were wearing them this past weekend?

BW: I hope so. I hope so.

JL: (laughs) Well, cool. This has been an honor having you on, and of course we'll talk more as we get closer to the seminar.

BW: Sounds good. Everybody better be there.

JL: Thanks for being on.

BW: You tell everybody they better be there, or I will hunt them down and smack them in the head.

JL: (laughs) You just did. I don't need to tell them.

BW: (laughs) Sounds good.

JL: (laughs) Thank you very much, Sir.

BW: Thank you, Sir.

JL: I'll talk to you soon.

BW: I'll talk to you. Thanks, Jeremy. Bye-bye.

JL: Thanks for listening to this episode of whistlekick Martial Arts Radio. Thank you to Mr. Wallace for taking the time out of his day to do this interview.

If you liked this episode, please subscribe to the show so you never miss out in the future. If you could help us out by leaving a five-star review wherever you download your podcasts, it would really help out. Those reviews help new listeners find the show.

You can check out the show notes with links to everything we talked about today, the books, the movies, and more, over at whistlekickmartialartsradio.com. While you're there, if you want to be a guest on the show, or you know someone that would be a great interview, please fill out the guest form.

Don't forget to subscribe to our newsletter, so you can keep up on all things whistlekick. If you want to follow us on social media, we're on Facebook, Twitter, and Instagram, all with the username "whistlekick." And of course, if you'd like to learn more about the great products we make at whistlekick, please check us out at, you guessed it, whistlekick.com.

Train hard, smile, and have a great day.

Sensei Fumio Demura

"When I met him in 1967, I was stationed in California. A fantastic individual. Very impressive. I remember in the early 2000's I introduced him to his first hamburger."

– Bill Wallace

"Fumio Demura will always be remembered for his outstanding teaching and contribution to the film industry. I've always been a fan of this legend who is one of the nicest, most humble Grandmasters I know."

– Cynthia Rothrock

"The first time I met Fumio Demura was shortly after *Perfect Weapon* came out. I was very impressed [by] how welcoming and friendly he was having never met me before and my clear subordinate role to him."

– Jeff Speakman

Jeremy Lesniak: Hello, and welcome to a very special episode of Whistlekick Martial Arts Radio. This is episode 130, and today we're speaking with Sensei Fumio Demura.

At Whistlekick, we make the world's best sparring gear, and here on Martial Arts Radio, we bring you the web's best podcast on the traditional martial arts twice a week. Welcome. My name's Jeremy Lesniak, and I'm the host and founder of Whistlekick Sparring Gear and Apparel. Thank you to the returning listeners, and welcome to those of you checking us out for the first time. If you'd like to see more about our products, you can do so at Whistlekick.com.

This episode is different from any that we've done. Demura Sensei is a private man, and his health isn't great. People that know him told me that this interview would never happen. It was only because of our profile of Sensei on episode 107 that this was even a possibility. The folks that produced *The Real Miyagi*, the documentary of Sensei's life, were kind enough to reach out to us, and ultimately introduced me to Sensei. This is the first episode we've released that's been entirely uncut. What follows is more than 30 minutes of stories and advice from Sensei, and within this episode, likely every bit of advice a martial artist could ever need. After all, who better to advise a martial artist than one of the greatest that has ever lived?

Sensei Fumio Demura: Hello?

JL: Hello? Demura Sensei?

FD: Hi.

JL: Hi, this is Jeremy Lesniak. How are you, sir?

FD: Okay.

JL: Is now still an okay time for us to chat?

FD: Yeah.

JL: Oh, good. How are you doing today?

FD: Alright. I just finished the dialysis.

JL: Yeah. How's that going?

FD: Oh, about two, three hours every day. That's tough.

JL: Yeah. Yeah. Is it painful?

FD: What?

JL: Is it painful?

FD: No, not too much pain. Just sit there too long.

JL: I'm sure there are many other things you would rather do.

FD: Yeah.

JL: But there are many of us that are happy that you're doing it, so you can keep doing the thing that we all appreciate …

FD: Yeah.

JL: … that you do.

FD: Yeah. I did two days with Black Belt Magazine. I just made a video for Kobudo.

JL: Yeah. I think it's great that they still have you doing things. I mean, that's how …

FD: Yeah, it was. I've done my best, yeah, to keep busy in my mind.

JL: Sure. What's the video that you're working on now? Is it on sai, or nunchaku?

FD: No, traditional kata for all weapons.

JL: For all. Okay. Wow. That's …

FD: Yeah. Sai, eku-bo, bo, kama, tonfa, and the nunchuck don't have any kata, so I made a kata that put them in there.

JL: Oh, okay. How many kata in total?

FD: About 13.

JL: Wow. That's going to be … And all on one video?

FD: I don't know.

JL: Oh, okay.

FD: That's their business, so I have no idea.

JL: Okay. That's a lot of work. Well, I don't know how much time you have. I wasn't sure if now would be a good time for me to ask you some questions, or if you just wanted for us to chat for a little bit, and then we could set up another time?

FD: Yeah, I can do as much as I can.

JL: Okay. Okay. So, our show, we have on a lot of different people, a lot of martial artists. Bill Wallace has come on. Dave Kovar. I'm sure a lot of people that you've known, and certainly a lot of people that respect you and learned from you, so I think a lot of people are going to be interested in your answers to some of these questions. We ask all of our guests the same questions.

FD: Okay. Just go ask me any questions.

JL: Okay. So, I've read a little bit about why you started martial arts, and of course I've seen *The Real Miyagi*, but when you started martial arts, when you were young, what did you think of getting to start martial arts? Was it something you were excited about? Was it something you were nervous about?

FD: Well, see, I started right to after World War II, just end the war, so we don't have any, no shoes, no clothes, no food, nothing. Couldn't afford no toys.

JL: Right.

FD: So, I had nothing to do. So, then one of my neighbors have a …
He's a Kendo Master, so I said I'd study in … Actually, not Kendo. We
call it Chanbara. It's like you cut wood into sword, and we have to fight.
So we have to make own sword, and then we go to my neighbor's, and
he showed me how to do it. That started it.

Then, after that, I went to my hometown [inaudible 5:19] Kendo,
opened a dojo, so I went over there. They were teaching karate, and I
would … Sometimes I read it, a book about karate, so I'm interested in
karate, but instructor said, "No, you're too young," so I couldn't get in
there, but I was watching every night. He said, "Are you interested in
karate?" I said, "Yeah." "Okay, come on in." That's why I was in there.
That's the starting.

Then, I have my friend, and he started same time, and he was ahead of
me, so I told him I didn't I didn't want to lose him, so I continued. If he
come at 2 o'clock, I go to 1:30. He leave 10 o'clock, I leave half hour
later at the latest. I never [inaudible 6:12] until back up with him.

Since I start doing that, in 1958, I think, I did the first karate tournament
at JKA [inaudible 6:28]. I was watching Mister Kanazawa and Mister
Mikami for the final. I was watching, so excite. That's it. That's how I
got to do it. I started that part.

Then, continue, continue, in 1961, first All-Japan, combined together,
they had a tournament. Shotokan, Goju-Ryu, [inaudible 6:58] all got
together. Then in 1961, I got the first place. That changed my life. I
wanted more martial art to do then.

Then I had a problem with my successor because I started to teach him.
He said, no, he can't teach this way, he has to do it this way, this way.
So, I decide I got to go to another county. I prove myself. Then, I meet
one, at that time, my friend and my martial arts friend, and he's well-
known Japan American guy, Donn Draeger.

JL: Yeah.

FD: He introduced me to Dan Ivan, and he wanted to study, so I started teaching him. Then, end of the section, and he got to go back to America. He said, "Are you interested in coming to America?" I said, "Yes, I do." Then, few months later, end up at the Tokyo Olympics 1964, and I heard, "Come to the America," so I said, "Okay." I just put them together. I came to United States 1965.

Then I stayed in a garage. At that time, karate, nobody knows. They call it Judo Chop. Anyway, we study, study, study. Then I do the demonstration for Kobudo, but nobody understands what Kobudo is. Then I started from there, keep going, keep searching different people, a different way, and then people talking about what karate does. I just create, create, create, and then I get big name.

Then that year, I went to Ed Parker's International Tournament and meet Bruce Lee at the demonstration for One-Inch Punch. Mike Stone was at that tournament. He received first place. Then I meet Mike, and they came to my karate club, and I started teaching him, and I made a good friend. That's what keeps going, going, going, going.

JL: Yeah.

FD: That's up to today.

JL: You've certainly had the opportunity to work with, I mean, so many wonderful people, and you just mentioned some of the biggest names that have ever been in martial arts.

FD: Yeah. Yeah. I'm real, real lucky.

JL: Yeah. clearly, you're very humble. You say lucky, and there are so many of us that look at what you have done and see so much hard work, and so much dedication to the martial arts. It's incredible, and it's a very inspiring story that you've just told, and one that I hope all of our listeners really appreciate. When you think about ... Sorry. Go ahead.

FD: No, it's okay.

JL: When you think about your time in the martial arts, your life as a martial artist, is there one particular memory that stands out as being the most exciting, or the best story? We ask our guests to tell stories on this show.

FD: Uh-huh.

JL: Is there a great story from your time that you would like to share?

FD: Well, I think it showed in my documental film, I was doing that Japanese Village. I did a karate demonstration, but people no react, no reaction, because they don't understand what karate is. So, I decide, if somebody punch somebody, when you're hit … Before that years ago, you punch them, they stop one inch before they're hit, so the guy doesn't move, but this way, it look like a hit. The guy move their head, punched in the stomach, bend the body. I go to this way, hit with the elbow, he fell over the side. Like a real fighting scene. That's why I started doing that, and the Japanese Village was a top show at that time, but Japan, they hear about I was doing karate for show. So, they have different kind mind martial arts people there over, over here. I already am more Americanized, so that's why I want to do it, I just did it. But I got a problem with Japan. Pressure, pressure, pressure, and I told to quit.

My mother said, "If it's something you're doing wrong, you can quit, but if it doesn't do anything wrong, just do it." I said, "I don't do anything wrong. It's just a different way I teach the public." "Then, that means they are jealous of you. They don't know anything about it. Just keep doing it." So I said, "Okay, I do it," and I did that 1974, I think.

For the World Championships, all the people come down from Japan. All the top Masters came over, and that includes my Sensei. That time, I put silver gi, not white gi, silver gi, and music on, and I did demonstration, and that time, oh, I can't put the music on, I cannot wear the silver gi, but then Dan Ivan said, "Just do it. Show it to the people."

So, Japanese Senseis about 1%. Other 99% is all outside countries of the world, so they have different mind, so I did it, and I got standing ovation.

JL: Yeah.

FD: That's why it saved my neck. Today, it doesn't matter where you go, even Japan. Every place you go, they do what I did 40, 50 years ago. Same demonstration, they do. Different than I do right now, but they can do the same way, so that's my improvement, and I'm proud I did it myself.

JL: Yeah, and there are a lot of people that would say that if you hadn't done your demonstrations the way that you did, martial arts wouldn't be as big today. How do you feel about that?

FD: That's right. Well, Japan, if you going down the bottom line, Japan martial arts people's mind is a little different than normal people. They have so many good things, but they don't use that things to [inaudible 14:37]. They think older systems run new things. Martial arts has so many good things today, but they don't use them, like we have a tonfa. We call them PR24.

JL: Right.

FD: Policemen use it, but Japan, nobody use it. Good things keep there, but nobody know how to use it, expect for today the police department. So, I started doing this. I taught them the introduction so that every country, all the persons in there study.

JL: What do you think it wrong with martial arts today?

FD: I think there's a lot of ego involvement.

JL: How do we fix that?

FD: I don't know. I'm trying to find out myself right now, but I don't know. I even might have some ego, but it's not ego. I proud of it, so I don't do anything people should not do those things. I think before I do. Some people just open their mouths.

JL: What do you think the best change, the biggest improvement, in martial arts has been in your lifetime?

FD: Well, in the martial arts it's said, "If you know yourself, and if you know other people, you have better chance to win. But if you don't know yourself, you don't know other people, 50/50. You don't know." That's why the way I learn. Before I do, make sure I know other people. I know myself, how much I can say, how much I can do it, but I don't make … say of myself big things. To me, I'm good guy or bad guy, I don't decide it myself. Other people decide. That's the way I learned.

JL: What does it mean to be a martial artist?

FD: Well, martial arts is basically self-defense, but I think, last 50 years I study, self defense, but I think more important we're called Budo. Budo, Bushido is development as better human beings. That comes first. They have a stronger mind, and strong body, then you can be a good martial artist. That's what I figure.

JL: Was there anyone, any martial artist that you wanted to work with that you didn't get the chance to?

FD: Yeah. If there's anybody ever been in my mind I want to go over there, I ask them, "Can you teach me?" I learned.

JL: Okay. Do you like martial arts movies?

FD: Sometimes. Sometimes people overdo advertisement. Overdo. But sometimes, I see the real good one, I like to watch it, because I study.

JL: What is the job of a martial arts instructor?

FD: Well, I concentrate to more young people, because young people are the next generation continue from my generation. So if you don't teach them, then martial arts gone, down. We don't want to go down. We want to go up. That means I have to teach young people to bring them up more better way to do martial arts. Right now, for example, I have over 50 years with me. Lots of people over 50 years with me, still with me, they're training everyday.

JL: Wow.

FD: So that's important to me. Not one year, two years, then goodbye.

JL: And how do you keep people engaged, excited about martial arts for so long?

FD: I'm not sure, but I want in this life direction, give the direction and keep interesting, the way I have to do that. Sometimes, it cost a lot of money for me. I got one guy said he don't have any money, but he want to buy the car, but he don't have any money to go in the bank to give it to them. So, I buy the kid's car, and I give you money, and when you have the time, just pay me back. You don't have to pay the interest, anything. Just pay me back. No contract, anything. I just give it to him, because this way, he trusts me. If he don't ever pay, he won, I lost. But I'm pretty sure most people, they don't have that kind of mind. They will pay. Doesn't matter what is.

That's what I want to teach. How to pay, then after pay, that's your car. Then next time, just sold this old car for down payment, buy a more better car. After little by little, you have to save money, you do that. So I teach them how to do it, because these people, they never learned. Parents didn't teach them. Thats a real big problem in this country, management money. So, little things, even not karate, but I teach the kids life.

Other people listen to me, they learn also same time. Sometimes, older than me, [inaudible 21:21], "Oh, you're stupid. You should not do that." But he knows he did the mistake, so that why he never fight me.

JL: Right.

FD: So he learned. That's why karate instructor is not just a punching and kicking teaching man. It's all other parts you have to be, teach, and you have to discipline yourself.

JL: Has the way you teach changed over the years?

FD: First time, 1965, and '68, to now, yes, I changed a little bit.

JL: What's different?

FD: I make more … Because I speak more English, so I can make a little joke about it, and then when I teach, I don't teach the mechanics. Okay, first time, exercise, same exercise. Then basics, kata, sparring, done. Finished. Not the way I teach. I teach the exercise. I do every day, I change it, make interesting the way. Other mean, students know exactly what I do next. That's no good. Make it doesn't know, so this way, students are more interested. That's how I teach.

I was in Japan, big problem. Japan, exactly teach kata, and basics, and kumite. Every day, same thing, over and over and over, which is good, but students know what comes next. Take the easy way. For example, we have to make the circle, and everybody's 10 punches, so he had to thinking, for 20 people, so 200 punches, so I got to shorten it a little bit, then can make 200. I don't do that. I do sometimes punch, harder punch, 20 times. Then, next day, I punch him harder punch 50 times. Next day, harder punch 100 times. Then people thinking, "Whoa, whoa, whoa, I got 100 times." Then next time I do 10 times. Okay, that's enough. Then they say, "That's it? I knew I should have put power." See? That keeps make interesting the instruction. That's how I teach.

JL: Which do you love more, teaching or being a student?

FD: Well, I like the teaching right now, because I can't move too much. Right now, only I can teach. But the teaching is very hard, but very interesting, especially teaching children.

JL: Do you like teaching children more than adults?

FD: Yeah. Children are more pure.

JL: Are they … Do you think they're easier to raise into good martial artists because they haven't been contaminated?

FD: Yeah, well, a lot of kids, they listen to me more than parents.

JL: There's a lot of responsibility in that. I've heard other instructors say the same.

FD: Yeah. Yeah, for example, one mother come and say, "My boy doesn't take shower. I don't know how to do it. I tell him so many times, he don't take shower." One day he came up here. "Hey, so-and-so-and-so, you stink. You go take shower." "Oh, okay." And he take shower. The mother happier.

Kids is always, whoever trust them, they listen to you. Every place I go, one thing, I make kids and me are sitting close together. Before I start class, I make the joke. it's not a joke. I say, "Listen to me what I told you. Okay, stand up. Sit down. Stand up. You did it too slow. Sit down, fast! Get up! Sit down! Up and down! Then, up." Then, next one, people think it's sit down. I say up. Then everybody sit down. People laughing. So, this way, "Come close, listen to me. Okay, let's go start class." That's how I start. The kids love that. Not too many adult people can teach kids. Some people, no patience.

JL: Is it just patience, or is there something else that people need to teach children?

FD: They need it. They need it. Every kid, they're looking for direction. But, I can't give everybody, so only I know, close to me, comes to the dojo, I can help. But otherwise, I can't help them.

For example, one kid … Kids in that first belt, from white belt to the color belt, first belt is very, very important. More than big money. So, the one father come up, and to buy the belt, it cost me $5. He said, "No, my son don't need a belt." I said, "You got to be kidding. $5. One drink, coffee drink, it's gone. You drink coffee. Why don't you save one cup of coffee, quit? Give it to kid. Don't be so stupid. You stupid father." He realized. He apologized to me. That kind of parents, we have too many. That's the way I teach them.

JL: Is there anything that people think about you? Are there any … What would you like people to think about you and your contributions to the martial arts? I'll put it that way.

FD: I'm not sure. I don't do that reason. I just do my job, what I need to do as karate instructor. That's what I do, so then later, they come up, that's a different story. I don't mean that way, trying to make that kind of way I do. No. I just does natural.

JL: Okay. What would you hope happens with martial arts in the next 50 years?

FD: I hope people have more loyalty, and study what is art. Art has no retirement. Like sai, you don't know how far you can, or nobody knows how far you can reach them. Same thing. Art, doesn't work. Only art is … That's enough for me. That's the end of the limit, so to me, I have to go until i die. I just do, stay martial artist. Some people say I'm retired. Thats end of it. I'm not retired, though. I sometimes joking about I'm retired, but I'm still working seven days a week, and I still travel different place, different people. I meet people, and I help people.

For example, I just came back from Utah. one little girl, born the wrong way. She needed medicine, but her parents don't have any money, so I did a little Miyagi. To the show, I charged money, and all that money go to her medicine. I give it to them. So, that's not for me, for all … I told them, "This is all from martial arts people. They donate to you. That's why I want you to keep up the appreciating all of the martial arts people." So, they understand. That's why I still teaching.

JL: Do you think you will ever retire?

FD: A lot of people say …

JL: I'm sorry.

FD: Huh?

JL: Do you think you will retire?

FD: I don't think nobody lets me do it. If I retire, I'm dead.

JL: I think many martial artists would say the same.

FD: Yeah.

JL: Many of the older martial artists I know say the same, that they can't stop. It's who they are.

FD: Yeah. they love it, so.

JL: Yeah. I have just one more question for you.

FD: Okay.

JL: We have a lot of people listening. What advice would you give to them?

FD: Well, whatever you do, do your best. That's my thing. Don't think for money. Don't pay, so do a lousy job. You pay a lot of money, good job. No. Doesn't matter what pay. You have to do a good job. What I mean is my philosophy is don't follow the money. Money come with you. That's number one. Number two, don't forget the beginning. Beginning, that's very important. Number three … Number three is … What was it? Oh. Don't give up. If you give up, it doesn't matter what you do. Nothing is good. If you started doing that, continue to do it, and you have to taking care of parents, because one day, your turn come up. That's the things I want your people to remember and that's part of the martial arts.

JL: Wow. Wonderful advice. Sensei, I really, really appreciate your time. Thank you for talking to me today.

FD: Okay. Thank you.

JL: Thank you. Take care.

FD: Thank you. Bye-bye.

JL: Bye-bye.

I can honestly say that speaking with Sensei as a martial artist has changed my life, and I hope that you gained some insight, or at least some enjoyment, from listening to our conversation.

We release episodes twice a week here at Martial Arts Radio - an interview on Mondays, and a topic show on Thursdays. You can find all of our episodes at WhistlekickMartialArtsRadio.com. You can follow us on social media - Facebook, Twitter, Pinterest, YouTube, and Instagram. The user name, as always, Whistlekick. If you want to know what's going on behind the scenes of the show, check out our sort-of-secret Facebook group, Whistlekick Martial Arts Radio - Behind the Scenes.

We're always open to new guests for the show, so if you want to throw your hat in the ring, or perhaps your instructor or someone else, head on over to the website, WhistlekickMartialArtsRadio.com, and fill out the form we have there. If you have any feedback, we'd love to hear that, too, and you can also send that to us on the website. If you like the show, please make sure you're subscribing. You know we're always asking for those reviews because they help us spread the word about the show, move us up in the rankings, and that helps new people find us. If you like what we're doing, this is the best way to help. Remember the products you can find at Whistlekick.com, like our great sparring gear.

That's all for now. Until next time, train hard, smile, and have a great day.

Don "The Dragon" Wilson

"One of the most fantastic friends I've ever had in my life. A superb fighter great at both kicking and punching. A very intelligent fighter."

— Bill Wallace

"Don Wilson is one of my best friends. What I love about Don is that he truly loves talking to his fans, and as a martial artist always willing to pass his knowledge to others."

— Cynthia Rothrock

"He is always a nice guy and a good friend."

— Fumio Demura

Interview was originally released on November 28, 2022.

Jeremy Lesniak: Welcome, everyone. This is whistlekick Martial Arts Radio, episode 766, and today's guest is Don "The Dragon" Wilson.

I'm Jeremy Lesniak. I'm your host here for the show. I founded whistlekick because I love traditional martial arts. I've been a traditional martial artist all my life, and I know I'm not alone, so we as an organization do a whole bunch of things for you, the traditional martial artists of the world.

If you want to show your support, well, you've got a lot of things that you can do. Start at whistlekick.com. Check out all the stuff that we've got going on. There is a good chance something we're doing resonates for you. If you simply engage, participate, purchase, that's all we need.

If you want the fullest experience for this or any other episode, go to whistlekickmartialartsradio.com. Yes, your podcast player on your phone or tablet does give you the show notes, but there are things that it filters out of the show notes, things that you're going to see at the website that you are not going to see on your little phone. Let's face it, most of you listen while you drive anyway. Whether you are watching this on YouTube, listening in a podcast player, the fullest experience you can get is at whistlekickmartialartsradio.com.

While you're over there, you can check out all the episodes we've ever done. You can sign up for our newsletter, you can throw us a tip … you could do all sorts of good stuff. Why might you do that stuff? Because we are working hard to connect, educate and entertain the traditional martial artists of the world, folks just like you.

If you want to support our work, let me give you a couple of specific examples. You could buy something, you could follow us on social media, or you could leave a review. Maybe you wanted to know that today's episode was coming up. The only place we release that information is in our Patreon, and that membership starts at just two bucks a month. There are also other tiers with all kinds of other good stuff.

Now, if you want the whole list, if you want, "Hey, Jeremy, where's the one place I can go and see all the things I could do to help whistlekick in the mission to connect, educate and entertain?" Well, it's the family page, whistlekick.com/family. Go there. You've got to type it in. We do that intentionally. If you're family, you're willing to take that small step. It's all the stuff you can do to help us out, as well as some stuff that we do not post anywhere else.

Today's guest, Don Wilson, many of you know him as a celebrated professional kickboxer. Many of you know him as a consummate actor, appearing in so many movies, but I have a feeling that most of you know him as both because he has been prolific in and out of the ring, on and off the screen. I was absolutely honored to talk to him today.

Hey, welcome.

Don Wilson: I'm happy to be here, finally. I apologize about … We had a problem … Well, I had a problem …

JL: It happens. It happens.

DW: … getting back to my office and then getting hooked up last time.

JL: It's all good. It's all good. You don't … You are nowhere close to the record for the longest time between when we started and when we finally got somebody on the show. I'm trying to remember who it was. There was somebody … it was five years.

DW: You've been doing this for five years?

JL: We're in our eighth year.

DW: Oh, congratulations.

JL: Yeah, thank you. We've been doing this for a while. It's been fun. I get to meet a whole bunch of people. Tons of your friends have been on the show.

DW: Hey, you know what? I haven't watched your show but …

JL: That's okay.

DW: Well, what is the official name, whistlekick or something or …?

JL: Whistlekick is our company. We do a variety of different things – apparel, protective equipment, we do events – but Martial Arts Radio is the show, so it's whistlekick Martial Arts Radio.

DW: Okay, well, then I have a very good reason to be here.

JL: You do. You have a great reason! Correct me if I'm wrong. Doesn't your daughter go to Middlebury?

DW: Yes, she does, Vermont. Yeah. She's graduating this year.

JL: If Vermont knew how to make roads that went east-west, I could be at the college in 45 minutes.

DW: Really?

JL: I'm in Montpelier.

DW: Really? Oh, wow. I bet it's cold where you are, then.

JL: I was just out walking in a T-shirt.

DW: Oh my gosh.

JL: It's like 61 … 60 … What does this say? It's not telling me. It's like 60 degrees out. It's great. Yeah.

DW: Oh my gosh. I'm in Los Angeles and that's one of the reasons why everybody likes living here is Mediterranean climate. We never get the ice and the snow and all that, but we had a drought for over 10 years. That has really messed up LA, the drought.

JL: I am worried. I keep seeing news articles about what they're going to do with the Colorado and everything.

DW: I'm looking right now … I'm in my office, this is my home office. I put it right in the front of the house so if I have anybody come over, they don't walk through, wander around through the house. They just come right in. The front door is right there, and I'm now looking out into the yard through the windows, and I have no grass. We purposely got a big yard for the kids and everything, and it's got an acre of yard, but an acre of dirt now.

JL: I have an acre and it's still pretty green. I mean, there are a lot of leaves down on it right now, but …

DW: If that's the only problem you have in living in California, then we're lucky.

JL: You're doing all right.

DW: Most of the things here are all positive. I actually have … My next-door neighbor is just leaving. People are leaving, though, because I guess, tax … it's financial reasons. It's expensive in LA, and I'm thinking it's property taxes or something. I'm not really sure what … why people are leaving, but I've had several friends leave.

JL: It's the whole pile of living there versus elsewhere. Vermont is …

DW: We come from Florida, and the people … My friend's here. He's a director. He's directed me two films. He moved to Florida, and he feels like … I guess he's getting his Directors Guild retirement or something, which is not bad, but it goes further if you're in Florida than it does in LA.

JL: Oh, absolutely. I think everything goes further in Florida.

DW: My boxing trainer went to Texas. My agent passed away a year ago, unfortunately for me.

JL: I'm sorry.

DW: I had him since 1985, one agent, and you know what? I thought well, I don't need an agent, but the reality is, you do need you … Here's the thing that agent did a lot of work for his 10%. He's on top of all the new films coming out before something gets made, like The Matrix, let's say. He knows there's a martial arts sci-fi being done by the studios, but me, I'm really like retroactive. If people really want me, then they just call me. They figure out … They find me somehow through people that know me, and they ask me to be in their films, and I do it, but that's no way to run your career.

JL: You've got to get there somehow, right? You can't start off …

DW: I've been acting for 40 years now, believe it or not. 1982, I did a Chinese movie … What was the name? *New York, Chinatown*. It wasn't a career move. I just appeared as a bad guy because I was very popular in Hong Kong as a fighter. I had six fights there, so they thought putting me in the movie would be good, and I was a bad guy, and I guess it was good for the movie. Then I just went back to my kickboxing then.

Then I met Chuck Norris, and he said, "Don, when you retire, move out to LA, get an agent, and be an actor." Chuck suggested it to me. He said it's a great second career, and that's what I did. I moved out there in '85. Of course, they weren't looking for six-foot-tall Asians with Southern accents – because I'm from the South, Florida – but, I get accidentally called in for a movie called *Bloodfist*. "Accidentally" because they were looking for a Caucasian lead, because they were trying to do something like *Bloodsport*. I don't want to call it a rip-off, but that's technically what it was, *Bloodfist*. It was just *Bloodsport*, but with me instead of Van Damme.

JL: They are really only three plots in martial arts film, so it's kind of hard to not rip off something that's already been done.

DW: Well, listen, I've starred in 30 movies now. I've done versions of other people's movies. I did a version of *Deathwish*. I did a version of *Under Siege*. Mine was called *Ground* Zero. Gosh, something just happened.

JL: That's okay. It was a little bit of a stutter in the network connection.

DW: Oh, you know what it is? People are calling me, I think. Yeah, that's what it is. You know what, though? I don't know how you run your business, but when I don't recognize the number, I never pick it up.

JL: Unless I'm expecting a call, I don't answer it, because it's always a scam.

DW: Well, I get a lot of messages left. They're trying to get me to buy a house or refinance, all kinds of crazy stuff. I only … If it pops up and I see the name, then it's somebody that I know and I do business with or have friendship with, and then I absolutely pick up.

JL: Sure. I want to go back to you being a bad guy in your first film, because that's something that I've heard anecdotally a lot of actors are really afraid of. They're afraid of being typecast as a bad guy and how that plays out.

DW: Maybe I should have been afraid of it, but I knew so little about the movie industry that I don't think I even … I may have heard the word stereotyped or typecasting, but I had never dealt with it. I didn't get into kickboxing with the idea that, "Oh, this is going to lead to a film career."

JL: Right.

DW: I didn't even think about it. Now listen, at this point in my life, in my career, I've played the good guy over and over and over. I'm not saying if someone's got a film, I won't be the good guy, but what's enjoyable is doing the different things. That's why we saw Clint Eastwood, at one point in his career, he did a comedy, *Every Which Way But Loose,* I think, or something. He had an orangutan in it. Then he did a love story with Meryl Streep. He just got so tired of being the tough guy that shoots everybody and kills everybody, and I know that feeling. Luckily for me, my agent told me … I got paid more to do one scene with Billy Zane than I used to to star in movies. I did a scene where I was just a Japanese businessman, no martial arts in it at all. It was in a science fiction … I don't know if it'll ever come out. It may already be out. I don't know, but when you just fly in, do one scene and fly out …

JL: Easy

DW: I may never see the movie. I don't know. Michael Madsen told me that he'll do 20 movies in a year. He doesn't watch the movies. He said, "Don," he told me about my career, he said, "You're leaving money on the table if all you do is star in one genre." I go, "What are you talking about?" Well, now I know. Now I know you can make as much, if not more money, just being what they call a "character actor." Going in, playing the bad guy …

JL: Sure.

DW: … playing the best friend. What I just did in … I guess was about three months ago, I got called to play an American Indian. Well, I better get it right. It's called Native American, because they don't like being called Indians, because that means they're from India. That's why the settlers called them Indians because they thought they were so dark, they thought they were Indian, they were from India, but you call them Native Americans. I played a good guy though, so there was no backlash. There were no Native Americans writing me on Facebook saying, "What are you doing taking a job away from a real Indian?"

JL: What, was it *Billy Jack 6*?

DW: No, no, no.

JL: I really want somebody to reboot that franchise.

DW: I don't know if it's politically correct, but some Mexican bad guys crossed the border, kidnapped some white women for sex trafficking, and go across the border. A sheriff … This is set in the West, the Wild West. A sheriff gets together a posse, but they need, of course, their Indian Scout to tell him where the bad guys went. I'm down there looking at the hoofs and telling them, "Well, they just left. We've got to go here," and I don't even know how to ride a horse.

They asked me in the beginning, "How are you with horses?" I said, "Well, I'm not scared of them. I'll get on one. I'll do whatever you want." The shooting was so fast, they didn't have time for me to learn how to ride. The scene is written that we'd ride up, three guys – the sheriff, and the other guy, and me – and we stop. I look at the ground. I point where we're going. I tell them, "We got to go this way." You've got to make that horse stop, move over this way, do this, and my horse had to be in the lead.

Here's what they do, though. This is in Arizona a couple of months ago. That horse only works with actors. That's what these horses … There's a facility in Phoenix were, I guess, everybody goes. All the stuntmen came from there. I've never made a Western, so I didn't know they have these areas of the country where just … Western towns, Western outfits, all you could ever want is right there. All you've got to do is fly in your actors from LA, put them in a hotel, and you're in Texas or whatever.

JL: Oh, what a riot.

DW: The horse, after two rehearsals, it knew what to do, and it just did it. My hands were on the reins, but I didn't make it go left or right. It positioned itself. It stopped. It hit the mark, right where it's supposed to. I did my dialogue. I looked at the ground and I told him what I was supposed to say. The horse was a better actor than me. Let's put it that way.

JL: That's a riot. That's so funny. I had no idea, but it makes sense. Horses are smart.

DW: They're trained.

JL: I grew up riding horses. They like to have a plan. They like to know where they're going. I totally get it.

DW: Well, his plan was, "Don't rely on the actor for the screen direction." We rehearsed it a couple of times. The horse knew what to do, and he just repeated it. I think it was a she, actually. She just repeated it, but that saved me, though because otherwise … I hope the producer is not mad at me because I guess I gave the impression that you put me on a horse and I'll just be riding, because I said I have no fear of them, which I didn't, but I didn't realize that it's not like riding a bicycle. You've got to learn how to ride horses.

JL: That could be the next Pixar film, a Western from the perspective of the horse actors.

DW: Well, you know what you, Jeremy, you probably won't see me in many westerns.

JL: You think that's it? One and done?

DW: Well, first of all, I'm Japanese. I mean, they probably should get a Native American. I'm sure there are some Native American actors, but you know what, though? I think the director had used me in another movie, and like I said before, I became what they call a recognizable name in show business. Not a box office star. I'm not Tom Cruise and Brad Pitt, but people recognize me, if they see … A great portion of martial arts action fans, of course, would. I'm 68 now. There's not a lot of … Stallone is reviving some of the older action stars with his *Expendables* – which, I'm trying to do something like that – but the truth is, action stars should be in their 20s to mid-30s. That's when I did most of my films, when I was in my mid-30s, but 68?

JL: It's never too late.

DW: There are roles like Liam Neeson in *Taken* …

JL: Yeah.

DW: … Denzel Washington in *The Equalizer*, Jack Reacher is a franchisable character that … not older, though. Tom Cruise is still pretty young, I guess. He's in his … Well, he's not a 20-something guy.

JL: No, he's, what, early- to mid-50s now?

DW: I don't want to age him. It might be late 40s maybe, but he's been around a while. I believe, if well-written, like … what was the one, *The Unforgiven*? Clint Eastwood was old when he played that, but he played it. You know what, here's what I don't want to do. I don't want to do the plastic surgery, and dye my hair, and try to play the 25-year-old kickboxing up-and-comer. I'll pay the coach, the trainer, the mentor to the kickboxer or whatever. There are roles that fit me and my age, but there's not a single kick or punch that I threw in the 90s that I couldn't throw today.

JL: I think that's an important piece. You look at a movie like *Balboa*, which …

DW: I haven't seen that.

JL: It's the sixth Rocky film. It's the one where he plays …

DW: Oh, it's another Rocky coming out? Wow. Yeah, *Rocky* is a great for that.

JL: Yeah, he plays with Milo Ventimiglia, and the whole premise is he's later in age. I don't know that they actually quantify how old he is, they might. He has to train and fight differently.

DW: Of course.

JL: He's going to go into this exhibition match.

DW: That's turning a negative into a positive, and Stallone would have done that.

JL: I think there's something to that. I've seen you on the mats. I've had the opportunity to be on the mats quite a bit with Bill Wallace, and seen a number of folks, your contemporaries, and as you said, there's nothing that you can't still do, and I think calling it …

DW: Well, I'm not the fighter I was, but I'm saying for movies, because look, Keanu Reeves can do his movies. Anybody can … I tell people I take no self-pride for my movies, as a fight scene, because you rehearse, you rehearse, and if doesn't look good, you just cut and you edit it out, and you get a different view. Those things are not like, "I'm proud that I did these fight scenes." No. I'm proud that I was a light heavyweight champion for 10 years, I held the title for 10 years, WKA. I didn't go out a loser. I came out of retirement my last time, won three more fights, and then I retired for the last time in 2002. I fought for 28 years, and that's a long career for a kickboxer.

JL: That's a long career, and it's inspiring, but I hope you don't underestimate the inspiration of movies, to see someone … Why was Clint Eastwood so popular so late? Because there are a lot of guys who aren't 20 or 30 looking and saying, "Okay, where's our representation? Oh, here's a guy who's been doing it, and we can aspire to be him."

DW: He gets behind his age. He turned it into a positive. He made his character … We couldn't see the bad guys. Do you remember that? He hands the gun … I don't know if you saw *The Unforgiven*, but he hands it to the black actor … you know who I'm talking about, but anyway, he couldn't take the shot because he couldn't see the guy well enough, so instead of being … Oh they did a movie about astronauts, where they got these old astronauts together. Do you remember that one? James Garner, I think, and Donald Sutherland, but anyway, you've got to take the negative things of aging and make it part of the script. Literally, like my character might not be as fast as he was, or you may not be as strong, but then he uses his internal strength to overcome the bad guys in some way, shape, or form. I think that's the way you work an older actor in an action film, is you let the positive … Well, I've got a script right now dealing with that. It's called the … well, it was originally called *Blood Rate*, but they changed the name to *The Dependables*. Obviously you know why.

JL: (Laughing) I have no idea why.

DW: It's like this: *BloodSPORT, BloodFIST*.

JL: Yeah.

DW: Now, you don't have to wonder what kind of movie mine's going to be. You don't have to wonder about *The Expendables*, because what it is, all the B-movie guys have agreed to do the movie, because we all know, if it's successful, we can do like *The Expendables*; we'll have a franchise.

JL: Can you share names?

DW: Yeah, I'm talking about Billy Blanks, Michael Dudikoff, Cynthia Rothrock, Richard Norton, Olivier Gruner. They've all said, "Yeah, we're on board when you get ready," and I'll tell you the gist of it.

JL: Please.

DW: It's a … We older actors are trained. We're the instructors at the SWAT unit for LAPD Police Department. We're training a couple of a group of young soon-to-be SWAT unit members. We go to the station, we're watching films and things, and all of a sudden, there's a terrorist attack in downtown LA. The real SWAT unit gets called, and they rush down to LA to handle this terrorist attack. Some bombs go off in downtown LA, and what happens is, it's a cover for a bank robbery. Hostages taken, lives at risk, I think two hostages have been killed already, or whatever, but it becomes then … so this is a life-or-death thing, and they can't pull the people off of the terrorist attack.

The old instructors are there with the young cadets. We order the young cadets not to come to try to help us, but they want to help us, of course. As old guys, we load up with our equipment, get in a van and we go to stop these bank robbers before they kill all the hostages or whatever. What ends up happening is, of course, the young guys come to help us.

They show up breaking their orders, and we chase the bad guys out of the building, and they run into an abandoned building, ready for a big shootout with us, and the buildings full of vampires. Now it becomes humans versus vampires, so the bank robbers and the cops join forces to fight the vampires. Yeah, I don't want to give away the whole story.

JL: That's quite a plot twist.

DW: Well, this is the idea of it. I was taught by Roger Corman. We did 12 movies together. He's the most prolific producer in history, with 300 movies, and I did 12 of them. I did more than anybody else. I think David Carradine was second with eight movies, but anyway … He taught me how to take an idea that has been successful for the studios, and then do a version of that and get a piece of that audience, because you won't ever make a movie that loses money because it's already proven that the concept is financially and commercially successful. This one is based on a movie called *From Dusk to Dawn.*

JL: Yeah.

DW: Tarantino wrote the script. He's in the movie as well. I don't know if you ever saw it, but it's a normal movie about these criminals trying to get across the border and go into Mexico, and they stop at a bar. At that bar, at midnight, a bunch of the people turn into vampires and kill all the humans.

JL: It's a classic. It's a classic movie.

DW: Right. Well, the structure of this is similar. When you start the movie, there's no hint whatsoever it's going to be a horror film in the end. It's a typical cop action thing with all these B-movie guys. I think it's going to excite everybody because everybody's on board, all the B-movie guys you ever saw in the 80s and 90s …

JL: Sounds like a lot of fun.

DW: … they'll all be in it, but they'll be in it as age-appropriate, as instructors at the police academy and teaching these young people that want to be SWAT. They aspire to be what we were, which was the real SWAT unit of LAPD. It's a Roger Corman concept. It's not going to get nominated for any Oscars, but it's going to be highly commercial because I believe the nostalgia … Look, *The Karate Kid*. They did the *Cobra Kai*. They got all the old fans watching it, because I watched the first episode which was great. I don't watch TV though, so I can't say. I kept following it, but I know it was successful. At one time, it was the number one show on Netflix, and that's an old concept, right? They got that guy Ralph Macchio on it . I think they even got Martin Kove. They dug Martin Kove up.

JL: Everybody.

DW: Well, they got them all back. If Pat Marita was alive, he would have been in it, if he was alive.

JL: Absolutely.

DW: I think this nostalgia has a value being you can't do the exact same thing you did in the past, but you can take some of the concepts of it, like our characters will all be heroic. In fact, some of the B-movie guys, I told them, though, there are only so many jobs the cops can do. The bad guys have to be also badasses, so several of the B-movie stars will be the bad guys, and they will not be in the sequels, just like Van Damme, I think, was the bad guy in one of *The Expendables*, right? He's not in any of the … I think … Did he get killed off? I'm not sure. I don't remember if he died.

JL: It's been a few years. My memory for movies isn't great.

DW: Their formula is not to expose the bad guys as action stars, and then use them over and over.

JL: What's next with this concept? When might we see it come to life?

DW: We are raising the money right now.

JL: Okay, cool.

DW: I was with the attorneys, literally, last weekend in Florida.

JL: Oh, awesome.

DW: Because the money is coming from a group of investors that are actually in … their music people, and they're in. Their idea is this, Don Wilson movies get – and they do, I get worldwide distribution. Every country, from Turkey to … I mean, weird countries, they all take my movies. If these music producers put their clients' music in the movie, their clients' music will be heard all over the world. That's hard to do with the music, but with my movies, instantaneously.

JL: That makes sense.

DW: We just have to make sure it's appropriate for the scene. I can't walk into a rap club and they're playing country western, so it's going to be … I never realized this. It's an attorney and a guy who's written … he's got maybe eight Grammy nominations or something. I don't know how many he's won, but they came up with the idea. I wish I could say … the financing of films … so they've raised up some money, and that's how we're going to make the movie. I told them, that's the movie we should do first is *The Dependables* because …

JL: It sounds fun.

DW: … in my opinion, it's for sure going to be a moneymaker, because of all the buyers from all over the world. I'm bigger in other countries than I am in American, by far.

JL: I've heard that, and I want to take that opportunity to go back. You talked about, I think you said six fights in Hong Kong.

DW: Yeah, and I fought in Berlin, fought in Rome …

JL: You managed to establish a fight career globally in a way that I'm not aware of people outside of … we've got some limited examples in MMA today. We've had some professional boxers over the years, but most of the people when we talk about fights and titles, it's North American-centric. How did you do that? How did you become global?

DW: Choose the fighter's hometown. If he's the main event, and he's from Miami, the fights are going to be in Miami. Vegas is the only place where actual fighters will uproot themselves and go and live there, because that's where their big fights are, Vegas. Here's what happened with me, and this kind of … many champions probably had the same thing. When I first won the title, other fighters around the world have promoters promoting them in, let's say Amsterdam and in Berlin. I fough the German champion in Berlin, the British champion in London, and the Italian champion in Rome. That's how I got my reputation, that Thai champion … in my weight division anyway … in Bangkok … I mean, I beat them in their hometowns, because I had to knock them out. I did not …

First of all, they were great fighters. Nobody put me up. Once you win the World title, you don't fight the easy guys anymore, the guys that are like 22-5 or something. No, you fight the undefeated fighters, or the number one contenders and other champions. I beat I think the number was 12 other World Champions, like Maurice Smith. I beat him. Dennis Alexio, the heavyweight champion, I beat him. "Oaktree" Edwards, world champion. James Warring, IBF boxing champion and kickboxing champion. I beat many other champions, as well as number one contenders, as well as top 10 fighters. I'm one of the only ones that …

Well, I was the First Kung Fu stylist to win a World Title in kickboxing. That's one of my claims to fame. Also, I lasted longer than any other pro-fighter. I started in '74, and my last fight was 2002. That's 28 years.

JL: It's been a long time.

DW: Well, for a sport where you elbow each other in the face.

JL: For sure.

DW: It's all striking. Look, I would have loved to have done MMA, because if the guy gets you in an armbar or something, you just tap out, and then no injuries, but my sport, there's no … we call that quitting. You're supposed to struggle and struggle and make him snap your elbow. In kickboxing, you fight 'til you're unconscious. There's no tapping out. That's called quitting. We call that quitting. When things are going south of the border for you in the fight, and you just go, "[tap tap] You know what? I'll fight you next month. I'm done tonight. I'm going home." We don't do that. We're expected to fight until we're unconscious, basically, then they forgive us. Listen, if you get kicked in the leg … I fought broken ribs, broken jaw, broken noses, broken hands. I had two broken hands in one fight, but if I just stopped and just quit and walked out of the ring, they'd be booing me.

JL: What's your mindset in a fight with two broken hands? You've got to be thinking about quitting.

DW: I tell people it's not good for my opponent. It's not good, because my mindset is … It's not the norm, because I was like a wounded animal. Now, they tell you if an animal's wounded, if it crawls into a hole, and it's got a bad leg or something, don't stick your hand in there, because it will … a wounded animal will fight harder, and that's the way I was. If I sustained an injury in the ring, my instinct is to give back more punishment to my opponent. In other words, that's like throwing fuel into a fire for me.

My whole career was 28 years, and believe me, I had fear in my heart
when I got into the ring in the beginning. First of all, we thought that if
you got kicked in the head, you might die, so it's a little scary. The first
full – we called it full contact karate. We didn't even call it kickboxing. It
was so new in America. It's 1974, and they had the first fights that PKA
put on, it was on TV. My brother saw that and he wanted to promote
the first fights on the East Coast, which was in Orlando, Florida. He
asked me if I'd do it and I said yeah, but we fought … First of all, we
fought on a concrete floor. Now think about it. If you get knocked out,
you're knocked out when you're up. Now my head is six feet in the air.
That means if I fall down, I'm going to bounce on that concrete with my
head.

JL: Right. That's a long way.

DW: Six feet. Now, if you drop a watermelon six feet, what's going to
happen when it hits the concrete?

JL: It's going to smash.

DW: Well, that's what would have happened to us. Thank God we were
so inexperienced, nobody knocked anybody out, because after that, they
fought on mats. Then after the mats, we figured out you don't have to
reinvent the wheel. Boxing already had a ring with an elevated platform
so people could see it better, because when you're fighting on a mat,
you're looking dead on it, you get a few rows back, you can't see
anything.

Anyway, we in the Professional Martial Arts Arena, Pro-kickboxers,
we're the first professional fighters in martial arts because they added
grappling and now we have MMA. You took kickboxing and added
grappling. Listen, there have been many kickboxing champions who
became UFC champions … I mean, not kickboxing, strikers, strikers like
Machina and Maurice Smith won the UFC. Strikers can … to translate,
you just add some grappling and then they become world champions.

JL: Absolutely.

DW: But you haven't seen a UFC champion get in a kickboxing ring and win the World Kickboxing title. It is not translatable because when you take away all their grappling, then … Randy's Couture got knocked out his last fight by a jump front kick, and I've been in kickboxing for my whole … since I was 18 years old, and I'm 68 now. That's 50 years. I've never seen a white belt jump-front kicked in the face and knocked out, so that shows you … Randy's a great fighter. I'm not saying he isn't. I love the guy. I consider him a friend, but his defense was so low, he was … both shoulders were square and he was crouching down. He's looking at Machina and Machina just looks up, just jump front kick, and knocks him right out. Jump front kick. You can reach a high level of MMA and still be vulnerable to strikes.

It's changing though, we're talking … How many years ago was it Machina knocked out Randy Couture? In those years …

JL: It's only a few.

DW: … a lot of strikers got success in the UFC, a lot of them. It's not like Royce Gracie. I never saw him throw a left hook or overhand right. The guys never … His punches are what we call arm punches. He extended them, but they're really not real trained boxing-style punches, and certainly no combinations. Royce never … didn't know how to throw an upper cut, a left hook. He could not mix punches up. That's the level … and he was dominating MMA, so that sport has gone from that to guys like … who's it? Silva? He's going to fight Logan Paul, I believe. Silva …

JL: It was this past weekend, Anderson Silva.

DW: Oh, Anderson Silva. Alright. I didn't even know … What happened?

JL: Paul by decision.

DW: Oh, he won by decision? Oh, okay. Well, Anderson Silva is a little … Paul has been in my gym. Logan Paul and Jake. Well, I think it was

Logan Paul. Logan Paul was in the gym. Those guys are big, strong, husky guys. They are on the level of beginning pros. They're not ... They were YouTubers, but every pro was something else before he was a pro boxer, right?

JL: They've been putting in the time, for sure.

DW: Right. They've got good guys around them, too. And you know what? They're not making nickels and dimes. When they come up to the gym, six cars line up, and it's a Corniche, it's a Rolls, it's a Jag, it's a Ferrari. That's how their entourage pulls into the driveway of the boxing gym that I trained at in Woodland Hills, and they're making money. I believe that he grossed $65 million when he fought Ben [Askren], I believe. He was a former UFC fighter/wrestler, and he knocked him out in the first round. I think Logan Paul ... The event grossed $65 million.

JL: They're pulling in a lot of money, and they're ... love them or hate them, love the business side of it or not ...

DW: I'm getting offers now. I'm getting offers to participate.

JL: It's pulling people in to a sport as spectators that would not otherwise watch it. People need ... they need a story. They need to have an emotional connection to somebody in the ring.

DW: This is a version of Championship Wrestling, but it's real.

JL: Yes.

DW: It's real. I really believe they are trying to win, their opponents. There have been recently a few boxing matches were some boxing people in the gym ... I don't train in martial arts gym. I train in a boxing gym, and they felt they were fixed fights.

Now, I'm going to tell you about the greatest fighter. I'm the biggest fan of his. I can tell you right now, I guarantee you it was a fixed fight. Fixed fights do happen. It's a business, and it's a money-making business.

JL: Yup. There's a lot of money.

DW: Muhammad Ali was a world champion. He decides he's going to fight Leon Spinks. Leon Spinks has eight pro fights when he fights Muhammad Ali. Ali fights them … I think it was 15 rounds. He goes 15 rounds. He doesn't have a fat lip, doesn't have a broken nose, doesn't have … but he loses the decision. He got paid $5 million. The rematch … In the rematch, he was guaranteed another $5 [million], so he turned that fight, and he knew … that's the one guy he knew he could beat. How could a guy with eight pro fights beat Muhammad Ali? And if you do, you've gotten really hurt, like … Ken Norton broke his jaw.

JL: Without a lucky knockout? Yeah.

DW: NO! With the distance he lost. Muhammad Ali lost the decision to Leon Spinks.

JL: Right. That's the point. Anybody can get a lucky shot, one in a million.

DW: That can happen, but that's not in this case. I believe Ali looked at it as a business decision. He said, "You know what, who is it I could fight, he's got a name, and people would pay to see it, and I could lose, and then get my title back one more time?" Leon Spinks got the phone call from … "Hey, you're going to fight for the World Title, Muhammad Ali," on his ninth pro fight. Because Ali … When you're a champion, like me when I was, I'd pick who I'd let get a shot at me and the title. I'd pick them. It's not that … I will say this, the number one contender, you have to fight them every year because you get pushed by the association, WKA. They're pushing and pushing because they know … Well, when I defended it against an undefeated fighter, Dennis Alexio, he sold that fight, the package, to NBC Sports World. That's a lot bigger than ESPN, especially back then in 1984 when we did it. ESPN, I fought the first fight on ESPN.

JL: Did you really?

DW: First fight, yeah, in 1979. I was … Then they liked it so much, they had a fight on every week, on ESPN, but anyway, I'm not going to say they forced me, but, yeah, they did force me.

JL: Encouraged.

DW: They told me I had to defend it. They'll strip you of your title. If you run from them. I don't think in one year, but listen, I didn't want to run from anybody, so I fought Alexio. I had the flu and I still fought him.

Oh. Sorry. My phone fell.

JL: It's okay. That's all right.

DW: We're back on?

JL: We are on. We didn't go anywhere.

DW: I was kind of pressured into fighting Dennis Alexio when I had the flu, and I beat him. Then he was offered a rematch with me. He turned it down. He gained weight and became a heavyweight.

JL: Why do you think he …?

DW: Everybody knew I was sick. Everybody knew I was sick, and I beat him, 12 rounds. We fought 12 rounds, and I beat him with the flu.

JL: Do you think that's why, this recognition that, "You know what? I can't beat this guy when he's got the flu. I'm definitely not going to beat him if he is …"

DW: Right. That's what I believe, because what I did was not physically beat him up, because you don't have to do that. It's a sport. You just have to score more strikes on his target areas, the body, and the head, and I kicked the legs. He couldn't walk after the fight. They had to carry him around. I kicked his legs, but there are rules in the fight as well. You have to throw eight kicks every round. That's what the rule was in 1984. Well, when you kick his leg, he couldn't get his kicks in. Two rounds, he got four kicks in one of them, and then I guess he missed two, so he lost the fight point-wise, just from not throwing enough kicks.

JL: That was your strategy going in.

DW: It was my strategy. I crowded him after I got my kicks in, and then I kicked him in the lead leg and I damaged it, so he couldn't really use his left leg basically. I'm not saying anything derogatory about Dennis, but I tell people I beat him with my IQ. I just out-thought him in the fight. The weakness I have, I overcame.

JL: Isn't that case with the best fighters? Don't people often talk about the best fighters as being very intelligent?

DW: Yeah, of course, dude. Yeah, he was. Well, Dennis was one of the better fighters though, so he was not stupid. He had a game plan like Tyson. Tyson, the bell rings, every round, he's going to try to knock you out, and guess what? Most guys he knocks out. Alexio, the same way. The bell rings, he goes forward and tries to knock you out. He's got 12 rounds to do it. That's his game plan. Nine times out of 10, he does knock people out, and that wasn't mine. If plan A doesn't work. I go to plan B. If Plan B doesn't work. I go to plan C. I would adapt, and they say Mayweather does that. Mayweather has certain things he does consistently, but he will crowd guys, avoid them, tie them up, he will use all the tools he has strategically to win fights over and over and over. He's been able to beat a lot of people, from Pacquiao, to Oscar De La Hoya, to all the guys he was waiting … You don't duck the big names because that's where you make all your money. You don't duck them. I didn't duck them in my weight division. I fought all the top guys.

JL: What made you come out of retirement?

DW: The money, and a lot of people said, "Don, that's … you're fighting for the wrong reason." I said, "No. That's the only reason."

What they did was this. They offered me … they called up … Well, first of all, they sent something that was from Revolution Productions. Now, you know I've been doing movies for years, so I thought it was a movie company, so I sent them information … They said, "We would like to discuss a business opportunity for you," so that didn't sound like a fight to me.

I sent it to my agent, and my agent calls up he says, "Don, this is not a movie." I said, "What is it?" He said, "It's a fight. They want you to fight." I go, "Fight? I haven't been in the ring in 10 years," and he goes, "Well, they want you to fight heavyweight," and the signing bonus, they called it, was $150,000, which means you get it when you sign the contract. Then, the offer is 12% of the pay-per-view.

Well, I had the same attorney that George Foreman had, so he knows pay-per-view. Henry Holmes is his name. I got him through Chuck Norris. Henry looks at the contract, and says, "Don, for a first-time fight on pay-per-view, this is a great contract." He says, "You could get millions of dollars." I said, "Well, I'm in," and at that time, I really didn't know Dick Kimber that well. I didn't know much about him because he's a heavyweight. He was up around 220, something like that.

JL: What were you fighting at prior to this?

DW: 175 is my weight division.

JL: Okay. That's a big difference.

DW: What I did was this, and this is a trick I used when I came out of retirement, and I might as well expose it now because I'm not using it anymore. I said, "Listen, I'm 175, you're 220. Let's meet in the middle. Let's meet at 195, cruiserweight," and that sounds relatively fair, right? I'll come up 20 pounds, 25 pounds. You come down 20 pounds. Well, it's not fair because I get to eat all I want, lift weights, and they, for the first time in their lives – heavyweights don't diet – he's starving himself, and basically all three of the guys I fought lost their weight with the rubber suit on, the sawdust, they dehydrated themselves. I don't know if you've ever done it, but I've done it. You drop up to 50% of your skill level. You're tired faster, your arms … Your body's going to heat up in the middle of the fight because, even though you drink the water right after weigh-ins, this is like 24 hours before the fight …

JL: It's not the same.

DW: … your body doesn't absorb it. Right. You're substantially … When I came out of retirement, yes, I was 48 years old fighting 12 rounds, but I was beefed up, full of water, full of protein, and I'm fighting young guys, 25 years old. Dewey Cooper is 25 years old. I fought him at the MGM. Solid muscle. He was weak as a baby. He was weak as a baby, so I can't brag about, "Oh, I won three fight …

JL: I would.

DW: Well, there's a fight in and out of the ring, right? I won by not cheating, but getting them to agree to meet in the middle was necessary. If I had fought Dick Kimber … I knocked him out in three rounds, but I believe at his 215-220, solid, eaten, lifting weights, it wouldn't have been the same kind of fight for me. Let's put it that way.

JL: No, definitely. It would have been a heck of a lot more difficult, but I love that there are some pretty well-established martial arts principles in what you're saying. Get them to fight your fight, if possible.

DW: Correct, right.

JL: Prepare, fight smart. We've got these threads coming through … Where did you ever take a fight you didn't think you could win?

DW: Never. Even when I had no reason to feel confident …

JL: Was that out of … because …?

DW: Even when I had no reason to feel confident, I always felt … Now listen, thinking you're going to win every fight doesn't mean you win every fight. I've got five losses on my record. Four of those losses, though, in my mind, I won those. It was hometown decisions. If you don't knock the guy out, I learned that early on, he's going to get the decision. You know, I thought the British champion in England, or London, German Champion in Berlin, the Italian champion in Rome. Do you think I'm going to get the decision? If it's anywhere close, there's no way. It's the promoter and they want me there just to build up their local guy. That's why I'm getting the money, but I said when the guy is laying on the floor, counting, and he's knocked out, there's no decision. There's no cheating you.

JL: I've heard it said, "There's no politics in a knockout."

DW: Correct, but it's a lot of pressure to have on you when the bell rings, because the guy is good, and they are good. Ferdinand Mack was a great fighter, and I ended up … in a 10-round fight, I ended up knocking him out in the ninth round, so that's cutting it pretty close. I didn't knock him out. A three knockdown rule was in effect, and I hit him in the body, which he was not expecting, because I kept all my punches to the head, tapping into the body a little bit, but I didn't concentrate on it. Then in the ninth round, I went down to his body. I dropped him three times, all body shots in the same round, and I won the decision. Now, I'm in Berlin with 10,000 Germans screaming, and all of a sudden, dead silence. He's on the floor.

Then, what was odd was that … This was 1989. I hear some cheering for me, and I'm thinking, "Well, who the heck are these Germans?" When I came out of the ring … It was before the fall of the Berlin Wall, and they were soldiers. We have American soldiers who were stationed in Berlin, and they were going, "Mr. Wilson! You won me a lot of money," because the German fans of this German fighter all bet the American soldiers that I was going to get my rear end kicked. The American soldiers, they didn't know me, but they bet on the American. I came out there wearing red, white, and blue. When I knocked him out, those guys collected their money. Their German Pro, what could the

German guys say? The guy's on the floor. You can't even argue about the decision. Anyway, it was a good feeling for me to get that pat on the back from our troops because they were winning money, because I assure you, if it was flipped the other way, like, "Oh, man, you just lost me a month worth of pay."

JL: You talked about why you took your first fight, to help your brother promote, but …

DW: Yeah, but I wanted to experience real fighting, too.

JL: Is that why you kept going in those early days?

DW: Look, yes, my brother wanted to promote it, but we didn't know if you could have a career like that. I was 18 years old, I was in college, I was an engineering major, and I lost my first fight. I broke my hand. It cost me more than I got paid. I got $100 from the fight, by the way, but the emergency room was more expensive to reset my hand, so I lost money, lost the fight, got injured, and loved it. It was so exciting.

People said, "Well, what's the difference?" I said, Well, we did point fighting. Everybody had point fighting. That goes back to the 60s, Chuck Norris' days, but that's like touch football compared to NFL. It's the feeling you get when you're a pro fighter, and you're actually knocking guys out, and you're in danger of being knocked out. The thrill, the excitement is lightyears beyond, like playing flag football with your friends. That's what it is. It's the difference between the Super Bowl and flag football with your friends. The point fighting was good. It does improve you to a certain degree, but it's not the same. It's not the same kind of dedication and enjoyment that you get from the sport that you get when you really are knocking each other out.

I'm sure these MMA guys liked the submission, because I wrestled in college, by the way. Of all the sports that I did, that was the one I took to the fastest was wrestling. I was the MVP of my high school football team, and the MVP of my high school basketball team. I ran track, threw the discus, the shotput, ran the high hurdles, sprint medley. I was an overall athlete, and I did in college what the athletic director said was impossible. He said, "Son," I said, "What sports do you have?" He said, "Well, we've got basketball, but the team's already picked." I said … because I had no money to go to college. I said, "What other sports?" He said, "Well, we've got wrestling. Do you know how to wrestle?" I said, "No, but I'll try out." He goes, "Son, nobody starts a sport at the collegiate level. Like the first day you touch a basketball, you're going for the basketball team. You want to try out for college basketball." Well, I had never wrestled, but the thing is this, I was an athlete, and my incentive to get that scholarship was my college degree. I was not going to be an engineer. My whole goal was to become an engineer like my father.

JL: How long had you been doing kung fu at that point?

DW: Two years, so I'd done kung fu. Kung Fu is not collegiate wrestling. It's a different sport. It's leverage. You've got to be strong, and man, we starved for each other, we dehydrated. That's how I learned to lose weight the right way, because I was doing it the wrong way in the beginning. I used to take E-Lax. Yes, and what happened was, I stopped because of this. I was sitting in a movie theater, and my back started hurting, and I'm 18 years old. My back was hurting so bad, I had to leave the movie here. Go to a doctor.

Now, when you're 18, you go to a doctor, you've got to really be bad off because we're invulnerable at that age, but I went to a doctor because my back hurt so bad. He couldn't figure out what it was. Then he says, "Tell me about your life. Tell me what you're doing," and I told him I was taking this Ex-Lax, and he goes, "Well, that's it. It's not you're back. It's your kidneys." He said everything's going through them, and you're destroying your kidneys, literally.

Luckily, I was 18 years old and everything, to my knowledge, I rebuilt everything. Everything's normal for me, but yeah, I damaged myself doing everything wrong to lose weight in college. That's why I believe as a fighter, I fought in four different weight divisions. I won world titles in four different weight divisions – middleweight, light heavyweight, super light heavyweight, cruiserweight.

JL: What's the bounds on that, for people who aren't fight fans?

DW: Generally, I guess you can say 10 to 15 pounds difference, each one.

JL: Okay, so the low on the middleweight is …?

DW: Pretty close. Super light heavyweight is close to light heavyweight. I believe, by the way, it was invented on the Dennis Alexio fight, because it was the day before the fight and he couldn't make weight. The promoter didn't want to cancel an NBC Sports World contract and all that money, and the promoter happened to be the association president, which is illegal in boxing. If you're the president of the association, you can't be a promoter, but now, Dana White, and now we just got thrown out the door. The actual association president invented a new weight division called superlight heavyweight, and he said, "You and Dennis are going to fight for that title." He said, "This is really good for you, Don," and I go, "Why is it good for me? I'm 173. He's 182." He said, "Because if you lose, you've still got your light heavyweight title. If you win, you get another world title." That's how the promoter sold it to me.

I looked at him, and I said, "Look, I don't want any other titles. I'm prepared to be sick, fight, and defend my 175, but now I've got to fight a cruiserweight." That's basically what Alexio was. What ended up happening is Alexia realized he's no 175 pounder, and he just gained weight and became a heavyweight champion. That's what he had. He just started putting on weight, because it's a lot easier to put it on then take it off, especially as we all get older, right?

JL: I haven't figured out how to get younger.

DW: Yeah, it becomes more difficult, so that's what happened with the Dennis Alexio fight, which … I never say anything bad about my opponents because that doesn't aggrandize me. They were good.

Warring was good. Maurice Smith. Branko Cikatic was first K1 when …
These guys were dangerous and good, and I still beat them, so if I call
them all bums, then I didn't do much. That's why I don't get that
mentality.

JL: Your time in the ring speaks for itself.

DW: Well, I don't understand the mentality of guys who put down their
opponents, say that they're wimps, and they can't fight, they can't punch,
they can't kick … why?

JL: Is it part of what we were talking about before, creating a story? Is it
part of the …?

DW: It's a promotion. They do it for promotion. I can't believe that
Conor McGregor really believed Habib was not a great fighter. You just
watch the guy. He's great, and by the way, he beat Conor McGregor.
Now, if he beats you, all the badmouthing you said about him makes
you look bad. If he's so bad, if he's such a wimp, and he's such a quitter,
why are you even fighting him then? I never did that, and Benny
Urquidez, I talked to him. I said, "Benny, you know how the fighters
badmouth each other today? I wouldn't feel comfortable. I don't have
anything personal against anybody I ever fought," and Benny said the
same thing to me. He said, "Well, you know, Don, they did make more
money than we did, because they've got on that championship roster."
He said, "But, I wouldn't feel comfortable doing it, either, just doing it."

JL: I think it's reflective of, at the time that you came in, and we've had
folks on the show who – Bill, and others – who were very …

DW: We were traditional martial artists.

JL: You were martial artists, first and foremost, and that attitude,
whether you were on TV or at a competition or just …

DW: We bow to each other. We don't spit on each other. You bow to
your opponent. You show him respect. You respect his instructor and

his style and his … It was a different time, and I know that it's promotional and more people are going to watch it. If you hear that I'm fighting Van Damme, more people will watch it if they hear us badmouthing each other. If I say what I really believe … Well, if I say what I really believe, he's going to consider it badmouthing because he's never had a pro fight as far as I know. He claims to be the World Champion, but he doesn't … In an interview, he said he couldn't remember the association that gave him his world title. How can you not remember? It's because there is no association.

JL: Every fighter I've ever talked to knows details of every round of every fight.

DW: Yeah, everybody knows their opponents … Frank Dux is going around, he's saying that he wants to fight me, but I've ducked him and all that. First of all, Frank Dux, he says he's 330-0, but he can't give you one name of one opponent because it's secret, he's sworn to secrecy, yet he made a movie about it. He can make a movie about it, but he can't tell you the names of his opponents.

JL: The way you mentioned the thing about Van Damme, is that something that might happen?

DW: Oh, absolutely. He's already agreed.

JL: Really?

DW: He's already agreed. Van Damme had a guy that he works out with contact me and say his guarantee to fight me was $3 million. If he gets $3 million, he'll sign the contract, and he will negotiate a percentage of the pay-per-view. That's up to him and his attorneys and his representation, but he will agree. He wants $3 million up front. It could happen, because let me tell you, we will sell worldwide. You know this guy Logan Paul, those guys? They don't sell in Germany and Italy and all over the world, but me and Van Damme would if … I'm saying the pay-per-view operators in those countries would just buy the rights from whoever has the rights to it in America.

JL: That would have a chance, if it was promoted right, of being the biggest pay-per-view of all time.

DW: Me and Van Damme fighting. They're doing eight rounds. Why not 12? That's what I'm used to fighting, and if he claims he's a World Champion, World Champions fight 12. I haven't heard him say it in a long time, but he did say it in the 80s, and it was even on one of the *BloodSport* posters, "Undefeated Middleweight Champion," and I tell people, he is undefeated. When you've never had one pro fight, you've got no losses.

JL: How would you prepare for something like that?

DW: Same way that I always do. Same thing. Cardio. First cardio, running six miles, nine miles a day. Jumping rope, I jump rope for an hour straight. I get my cardio up because I don't have to learn anything. Watch him fight, he's got no fights to watch. I don't believe that stuff anyway because, you know what? If you think … If you're worried about the guy's right hand, you see he's knocked out six guys with the right hand, he might … while you're looking for that right hand, he might throw the left hook and knock you right out, so I don't put a lot of stock in the pre- …

In self-defense, if a guy throws a beer at you in a nightclub, how much time do you … how much do you know about his fighting style? Nothing, so as martial artists, we have to be able to go from zero to 100 miles an hour. I just took that with me into the kickboxing ring. I watch him a little bit, but for me, the actual experience of being in the ring with them, checking how fast they are, their reflexes, that means more to me.

I can analyze the fighter faster that way than studying them and spending 100 hours watching tapes. In the first couple of minutes of the fight, I'll know everything I need to know because we have a feeling-out process. Most experienced fighters, guys like Benny Urquidez, they say oh, they're slow starters. No, we're going 100% in the first round, but I'm doing more watching than I am striking.

I tell people I throw up a smokescreen. They go, "What do you mean smoke screen?" I say I'll throw stuff, the guys think I'm trying to hit them, and that is not what I'm trying to do. I will do that for three or four rounds. I call it Rocking the Baby to Sleep, because by the fifth round, the guy hasn't been stunned. I haven't hit him with a solid body shot. I haven't stunned him. He gets a feeling like he's safe in the ring, and that's how I knock guys out. I've got 48 knockouts. Most fighters with 48 knockouts didn't say, "Oh, he's a knockout fighter." Marciano, I think he had 49, but people call me a technician, because during the fighting, I don't get punched in the face.

I've had 12-Round fights where the leather of my opponent's glove never touched the skin of my face. I don't take punches to give them. I come from the traditional point fighting where you don't let a guy touch you. When guys crowd me, I close the gap. I go closer to them, because I tell people, if you step back … like against Branko Cikatic, everybody ran from him because he knocked out 20 straight guys. If you go away, he's used to going forward, he could still put as much if not more power into his punch, but I would start to step back, he would step forward. Then I moved forward, and when … it was like a 1-2-3. I stepped back, he comes forward chasing me, and then I came forward on that third move. He's thrown off. All of a sudden, he's ready for that big right hand and my head is here on his chest.

Now, for a split second, he's disoriented, and then that's when I was landing punches raw on him. He was Undefeated European Champion and I knocked him out in the seventh round. It took six rounds to rock that baby to sleep. When he felt comfortable, he charged me, put me up against the ropes, threw three right hands. I threw a right hook, ruptured his eardrum, broke his jaw. When he hit the ground, he broke his nose. One punch

JL: Is there anybody from that era that you wanted to fight but it didn't happen?

DW: Many. Many.

JL: Any names that we might recognize?

DW: I had a fight offers with Rob Kaman. Rob Kaman was a great fighter. We should have fought. We were in around the same weight division. They offered me a fight with him, but it was less money than I was getting to fight easy guys in America, so I said no, the money's not right. If the money had been right, I would have gone, fought it, it wouldn't have mattered because like I said, my ultimate goal as a martial artist was to improve myself as a martial artist. Fighting the best guys is how you improve.

Now secondarily, I want to make as much money as I can. That's the reason why the fight with me Rob Kaman … I will say this. Ernesto Hoost, I didn't fight him. He's one of the guys. He was called Mr. Perfect, he was one of the K1 champions. Ernesto Hoost fought Branko Cikatic and got knocked out twice. I didn't feel as much pressure against Ernesto because I said I knocked out the guy that knocked him out.

Once, he was in England. We were in England together making appearances, and he goes, "Why did you back out of the fight with me?" I said, "What fight with you? I never agreed to fight you." He goes, "They had the posters printed and everything." I said, "Well, okay, somebody might have printed some posters, but I've never had a fight with you to back out. Why would I back out with you and I knocked the guy out that knocked you out twice?" I sent it right through the big crowd. He had nothing to say. There's not much he can say, right? He got knocked out twice by Branko Cikatic. Branko Cikatic got the courage to come to Florida and fight me in my hometown, Orlando, and I knocked him out.

Now, if I'd have just won a close decision against Branko, there'd have been a question … To this day, people would be saying that maybe Don didn't really win, and maybe he did, because of the local judging and all that kind of crap, but when the guy is … Like I said, when the guy is … Well, it's not a nice term. I used to call it flopping like a fish on the floor, there's no argument. There's no argument, and there wasn't for Branko.

JL: Who is your favorite fighter to watch?

DW: Jean-Yves Theriault.

JL: Why?

DW: Great defense. Everybody talks about his offense, and he has probably – I don't know, you could check this, Google it, maybe – he probably has the best knockout record in the history of kickboxing, Jean-Yves Theriault, but that's not the part of it that … His defense was great. He never … He's like … if you've ever watched Alexis Arguello. Alexis has worked my corner before. I knew him from Miami, where he lived in Miami.

Jean-Yves Theriault had a great defense, didn't take a lot of punishment, and knocked a lot of guys out. Under his rules, the rules that he fought under in full-contact style, he was probably the best. Now, I fought him and they called it a draw, 12-round draw. I felt I outpointed him, but under that style of fighting, especially since my fight just before that was a Thai kickboxing match in Hong Kong two months before.

I did something he didn't do. I went and I fought Muay Thai, Japanese kickboxing, and full-contact style, which is the Western style. He was better than me at that, I believe, even though they called it a draw, even though I did feel like I outpointed him, consistently he proved that's the style of kickboxing he's good at, the style where it's only above the waist because he could concentrate on his hands and mainly his right hand.

Now, when you throw the right hand, you don't have your weight on the back foot. It's sitting in that lead leg, so as he's throwing it, if you kick that lead leg, you do the damage. If had fought in Thailand, that's what they would have done. They would have thrown twenty kicks every round at his lead leg no matter what he tried to do. Just think about it. If your back leg … your weight is there, you can't throw a real right hand. The weight is … yeah.

Jean-Yves had a certain set of rules that he was the greatest at, and it was the full-contact style. I will relinquish that style of fighting to him. Some people call me the greatest of all time and all that. You can't tell any of that stuff. That's all conjecture, it really is. It's fun for people to argue about.

JL: It is. It is a lot of fun.

DW: Unless you really fight, you don't know what would happen, right?

JL: Yeah.

DW: Ali used to say this. Ali used to say, "I'm the greatest. You know why?" I'd go, "Why?" He goes, "Because if I fight you 10 times, I'll win six out of 10." He's not saying he would win every one, and I believe that about Ali, don't you? There's not a guy in his day that would beat him six out of 10 times. He would figure them out. He would outsmart them by the second or third one. He might make a few mistakes, then he'll correct them, and then he'll beat you. He's got certain things that he can do better than anybody and that was moving around the ring. To this day, you don't see lightweights moving like that.

JL: No.

DW: No. On the balls of his feet, just dancing around the ring.

JL: He was fast.

DW: Yes. Then what he would do was plant, he'd score with the left hand and knock guys out with right hands. He didn't have the big uppercut like Forman, and he didn't have the big left hook like Frasier. He had the right hand, but he hit guys right on the chin. He hit on the chin so much, they said it was a phantom punch, like with Sonny Liston, but it's not. Real fighters know, I know. It takes very little to knock somebody out if you just land right there, and the gloves Ali wore were the gloves that I wore in the 70s. They're horsehair. They're not foam padding. They're literally … If you cut them open, there's hair in there, and supposedly it came from a horse and that's what they stuffed them with. That is … It protects your knuckles, but it really translates into a hard shot on the chin. They used to have huge cuts on guys like Marciano, cuts that run across their noses and stuff because those gloves are different than the gloves we use today. It's not that they hit harder then. They hit hard today, as much as then, but the gloves protect … I think … Who wants to lose a fight on a cut? I got head-butted accidentally one time.

JL: Who wants to win a fight on a cut?

DW: I don't. I don't, but I got to cut myself though once and it was all coming into my eye. I couldn't see out of my left eye at all. The referee came over there and took a look at it, and I thought they were going to stop the fight. I was thinking I'm going to lose my world title. I'm way ahead on points. I'm not saying the guy's a dirty fighter. He accidentally head-butted me. I'm pretty sure, no, 100% sure he accidentally head-butted me. It might have been something that I did because, like I told you, I like to close the gap, so I was probably trying to get in real tight and we bumped heads, but it was going right directly into my eye. It's weird, all of a sudden, you lose your depth perception because you've got only one eye. You know how you think, "Oh, it's going to go black?" To me, it's like grey. It was weird. I never had blood cover my eye where I couldn't see, but that was 1990.

I retired right after that fight because I was afraid. "You know what? I'm doing these movies, and I don't need the money." In fact, the time that I would take to get in shape to fight back then, I'd lose money. When you do something and you lose money, or it costs you money, it's not a career. It's called a hobby. Kickboxing, because it wasn't making me big money, and the movies, because it was …

JL: It became your hobby.

DW: I've made millions of dollars as an actor, believe it or not. Of course, I spent it like everybody else, as fast as you possibly can.

JL: Well sure. You've got to keep the economy going.

DW: But even at the B movies, I would do five movies a year, and you can do the math. I was getting $220,000 per film – $20,000 would go to my agent, I'd get $200,000 – and they all made a profit because it's all about video, and the videos were being rented. People would go every weekend to the video stores to see what they were going to watch that weekend.

I had five movies in 13 months I released once. Shot and released five movies in 13 months. *Entertainment Weekly* came to me and said they wanted to do an article because, to their knowledge, no actor in America had ever done that, but video didn't exist, right? That's why. Tom Cruise doesn't need five movies in 13 months. Actually, they were calling it five movies in a year he shot and released, but it wasn't really that, but *Entertainment Weekly* said that. It was 13 months, but they were all shot in one year, but one of them was released the next year. Nobody does that.

Now, as a character actor, you can appear in 20 movies, like Michael Madsen will do and Eric Roberts, but to be the star of one genre, like all martial art movies, which they were for me, that's all I starred in. If I'm not kicking, I'm not in the movie.

JL: Let's say we've got somebody who doesn't know your catalog of films, or maybe somebody younger. What movie should they start with?

DW: *Red Sun Rising.*

JL: Okay. Is that your favorite one that you've done?

DW: It's an HBO World Premiere. I did four of them. It's got a little of everything. It's got a love story. There's a female cop, there's a relationship. It's got good character actors, Mako and Michael Ironside, and Edward Albert. It's just a well-made movie. The director was very experienced. He's passed away, but he was a British director, and he came here and that was the first movie he did in the US, and he just did a great job.

Now look, I'd like to take all the credit, but I did what I normally do. I memorized my lines and I gave my performance. Directors adjust them. Maybe they might say, "Hey, you know, you're coming off too strong there. You need to back off a little bit, or …" Directors director your performance, so if you see a movie, and you hear a guy wins an Oscar, go look up the director because that actor is given the performance the director … unless you're Tom Cruise because you can just tell the director, "Hey, this is the way I want to do it." I heard he did that to Spielberg, by the way. Spielberg had a scene, he told Tom what to do, Tom said come over here, and they supposedly … and I'm hearing this from the stuntman. The stunt man, he was behind an airbag, and next to the airbag, they didn't know that the stuntmen were hearing them. Spielberg was telling Tom Cruise why he thought he should do this certain thing in the scene, and Tom said, "Look, my character regardless, my audience does not want to see me like that." Now, I don't know whether it was crying or what, he said, "My audience does not want to see …" Now, this is Steven Spielberg.

JL: Can you imagine being such a big actor that you can tell Steven Spielberg, "Thank you for your notes, but these are unnecessary."

DW: Right. Well, they're not coming to see Spielberg.

JL: It's true.

DW: That movie was called … It was the one with the aliens coming to Earth. *War of the Worlds.*

JL: Yeah.

DW: He did the remake of *War of the Worlds*, and that was … the one Spiel- … Yeah. I was told this by a stunt coordinator. He said, "We were behind this airbag hanging out and laying there, and we heard Spielberg call Tom Cruise," because he's not going to do anything like that. They're not going to have a discussion like that in front of the crew, so they thought they were alone. He brought that up because we were working together, and he was directing me in a movie. He was trying to say, to me, he says that he knows that in the end, it's me that my audience is coming to see, but you know what? I relinquish any power I have on movie sets because there can only be one captain of the ship and that's the director. I try to give the directors what they want. I rarely have had any … There is one time, though. There is one director, one time. It's the only movie I made that there are scenes in the movie I'm ashamed of.

JL: You don't have to name it if you don't want to, but I'd love it if you did. Which one?

DW: It's a movie called *Blackbelt*, and here's the reason why I don't like it. I know what happens. If I say the name of the movie, everyone says, "I'm going to go see this movie. This is the one movie Don Wilson regrets," but I called the director the Twilight Zone director. We got into an argument on the set. He wanted me to kick my foot, the point my boot, closer to the other actor's face. I said, "Wait a minute. I'm not … This is not even safe what I'm doing. I'm not going to get closer to his face. You move the camera six inches to this side, and then it won't show …" He had the camera here and I'm throwing the kick so you could see the space.

JL: Right. Change the angle.

DW: It was the angle, and the name of the actor is Matthias Hues, and Matthias Hues is the gutsiest nicest guy you will ever meet in your life because he just trusts me not to blind him with my … I was wearing a cowboy boot. It has a point on it, and the director wants me to get that closer to his face because it looks like I missed because he's got the camera in the wrong spot.

JL: Was it his first martial arts flick?

DW: That director wrote a script. Now, the only reason he wrote the script is this. Roger Corman comes to me and says, "Don, what movie do you want to make, and who do you want to direct it?" I tell him … this guy. I might as well say it. His name is Chuck Moore, and the movie is called *Blackbelt*. I think, he's a screenwriter, he could write the script and direct it. I like him, and I believe we should. I got him the job, that's the thing.

He comes to me and he says, "Don, I'm not changing anything in this script because if they didn't think I could do the job, they wouldn't have given it to me," and I'm thinking to myself, "I'm the one that gave you the job, and you're telling me I have to …"

The scene was this. There's a guy, a serial killer, that's Matthias Hues. He's a big, tall blond guy. I don't know if you know him as an actor, but he's well known. The director says we have to show why he's killing women. We have to show the reason. I said, "No, you don't have to show. Why did Jaws eat all those people on that island? It doesn't show that the shark's swimming around. He can't find enough fish, so he starts …" The character, the bad guy is defined by his actions. He's just an evil man because he murders women. Why he does it … Why does Hannibal Lecter eat people? They never have a scene where you see him … slowly …

JL: He thinks they taste good? I don't know.

DW: We don't know, because they didn't show anything like that. He's defined by what he did. Now, he was a scary bad guy, Hannibal Lecter. This guy's a scary guy, and I said, "He kills women. We don't have to show why," but the director wrote a scene where he's got this young kid sitting on his mother's lap, and she's saying, "I'm going to make you my little husband." He was sexually molested by his mother. He grows up hating women, and that's why he's a serial killer. It is a very distasteful scene, and if you're ever going to show anything like that in a movie, you should do it the way Jodie Foster did with … There was a rape scene where a girl gets raped on a pool table, and it's based on a reality thing. Jodie Foster was directing it, and you do it for the right reason. You don't use incest as a …

JL: It has to move the story forward. If it doesn't move the story forward, there's no point.

DW: Well, you know what, to me, it stopped the movie dead in its tracks. It didn't do anything … it didn't sell one more ticket. People aren't going to say, "Oh, well, we don't learn why he kills women? Well then, I'm not going to rent it." It's not like that.

Anyway, that director and I never worked together again. Most of the directors, I've done multiple films with them because we get along, but I have what they call Mutual Approval Contracts. In other words, every aspect of filmmaking, if I don't want to do it, I don't have to. I didn't like the scene, but I have never enforced that. I've never forced some director or producer, including this guy. I never forced … I told him, "This is what I believe. We should just cut that scene out." He didn't agree. Kept it in. I have never enforced it, but I keep it in my contracts because just in case.

Oh, there is a scene. I'm not going to tell you this director's name, though. He wants me to do rear nudity in a movie, because I guess Van Damme did it once. I don't remember. Nobody wants to …

JL: I think Van Damme did it more than once.

DW: Okay.

JL: People like seeing his butt.

DW: He was the number two or three actor in the gay community when he was doing *Bloodsport* and *Kickboxer* and all those, which there's nothing wrong with that. You can be popular for the gay community, but if you show your rear end, I mean, you get …

Anyway, I told the direct … What he wanted me to do was this. Well, I'm in a whirlpool, and he said, "You'll just reach for the towel," so he said, "There's nothing sexual about it. You're not going to be having sex." I'm thinking to myself. I said, "You know what? There's not a single person renting my movies," because back … you know, video, "That's going to say, 'Oh, Don Wilson shows his butt? Oh, I'd better get this one. Oh, Don doesn't show his butt? I'll wait for the next one."

Nobody's renting my movies to see my butt. I said, "They're renting them to watch me KICK butt." That's what I told the director, and I cut that scene right out of the movie.

JL: That should be on a poster right there, that phrase.

DW: They don't pay to see my butt. They pay to see me KICK butt.

JL: There's your movie poster for your new film.

DW: That's a true story, and it's about one of my movies. Yup, I didn't show my butt in a movie.

JL: Wow, this has been a ride. I know you're on social media.

DW: Yeah, Facebook. Facebook if you want to …

JL: If people want to follow you, and stay up on what you're doing …?

DW: Oh, Yeah. Listen, when I travel around, I take pictures. I'm not like Cynthia Rothrock. She is meticulous about it. It's like a job for her. You should be getting paid putting all this information out, but I do, I put it on. I talk to people all over the world and I enjoy it. I like being in contact with my friends through Facebook. I was in Iraq a couple of years ago, and called my wife from the hotel. It's free, FaceTime. I could see her. When we had the shut down, I was in Iraq, signing the black belt of the President of Iraq's nephew or something. Anyway, that's …

JL: That's cool.

DW: It's weird the things you do.

JL: Yeah.

DW: Well, the President of Chechnya invited me, Mayweather, and Mark [Costa] to his birthday party. We all flew there to his birthday party. He's a big fight fan, the President of Chechnya. I don't know what's going on now but I think … Gosh, Putin's causing so much trouble in that area because I did eight seminars in Ukraine about a year ago, a year and a half ago. Ukraine is just like Russia. It's like we rode tanks into Canada because we don't like something they're doing.

JL: I'm going to ask that we draw a hard line there. I try really hard not to let politics come in.

DW: No politics, right, right, right. But anyway, I was in Ukraine, and I taught seminars there, and great people, just like the Russians. I go to Russia, and I'm very popular there. Their people are just great people as well.

JL: Two more questions for you. First one, if you could go back now, you could get in a time machine and go back to let's say 18, maybe right around that first fight, and talk to 18-year-old you, what would you say?

DW: Well, I've made some mistakes as a fighter. One of them is, it's not just a saying that anybody can be knocked out at any time by anybody. The worst opponent you ever face could still knock you out if you're not careful, because that actually happened to me. It's not just hearsay. The guy's record was 9-6. He knocked me out in the first round. He had three more fights … Now his record is 10-6. He had three more fights after that. He got knocked out on all three, and he retired with a 10-9 record, so the fighter with the worst record knocked me out in the first round. It's not a saying for me to say, "Oh, anybody that …" He was called a tune-up bout, first of all. The tune-up bout knocked me out in the first round. I was TKOed, went down, got up, but I was too dizzy to fight. I would have told myself, you got to keep your defense. Young fighters come in the gym and I say, "Listen, defense first. Make sure you're not going to get hit." Oh, sorry. I apologize, I forgot this phone is on.

Answering Machine: Hello. Please leave a message after the tone.

JL: I love that it's going full circle, right? We talked about this at the beginning that it's always a scam. Defense first.

DW: Defense first. I wish somebody told me that first day. Now, I learned that. I don't remember when in my career, but I made it so that my opponents would not score on me. Therefore, it took all the pressure off my offense. If you go through a round without being hit, all you've got to do is land two jabs to win that round. That's one thing.

The other thing is, it's very easy to knock people out. All you have to do is hit him with a punch they're not expecting. That's how you knock people out. If the guy's ready for it, and he's all … you're not going to knock him out. You're going to hit his head, knock him around, but you get him to … I tell them, you get him to look at Hekyl, and you hit him with Jekyl. That's a very simple strategy. Throw kicks high, and then you drop down low, throw a body shot. Kick low, and then come over the top with an overhand right and knock the guy out. Setting people up. You get them thinking one thing, like misdirecting them, get somebody to look at … Well, the matador with the cape. The bull looks at the cape, not the guy's body, and he gets mad and he goes for the cape and he keeps missing the guy.

That kind of strategy doesn't just work in bullfights. That works in the real fight game. There's a reason I keep my one hand down. I keep it down because it looks open. Guys try to throw overhand rights when … I'm South Paw. They try to hit South Paw with right hands, and I counter it with my sidekick to the body. I'm thinking two moves in advance, and like a chess player, you've got to think of few techniques in advance, maybe even a few rounds in advance.

This is a coincidence that … It was not my planned strategy, but it worked out this way. My last fight was a 10-round fight. I could not throw right hands because I had fractured my rib the week before the fight, so I was afraid if I threw the right hand, that would expose all this.

The guy might kick it, he might hit it, so I kept my right hand here the whole fight. It's the 10th round and I'm not winning. Both my Corners are saying, "It's close, and it's his hometown, Atlantic City. He's the main event here many times, you're not." My trainer said, "Look at this crowd," and it's a sold-out crowd. He goes, "If he gets the decision, there's not going to be any booing. He's going to be cheered out of here because it's a close fight and he's the hometown guy. You've got to knock him out. It's the last round, the 10th round. You've got to knock him out."

I stood up and I thought, "Well, you know what? I might as well throw the right hand now." It's the last round, might as well. Think of it, he had not been hit with a good right hand the whole fight, so his left was down. I took nine rounds to set him up. Not purposely, though. Nobody would have the patience, or the guts, to wait nine rounds before you throw the right. I threw the right hand and knocked him out. The ring announcer gets the microphone, "Ladies and gentlemen, winner by knockout in the 10th and final round with four seconds left on the clock." When I told Holyfield that story, he burst out laughing because if you had given me a script that said that, I'd say, "Nobody's going to believe that." It's a close fight, he's probably going to lose it, and he knocks him out with four seconds? But that's my life. That's a reality for me. My last fight I won in the last four seconds.

JL: I love it.

DW: You set guys up. The moral of the story is, you were asking for techniques that I would have told myself? Pick your time. Set guys up. Don't wait until the last four seconds though. That just worked for me, but generally, you've got to have defense first, don't get scored on, take some pressure off your offense, and then when you use your offense, you get the guy thinking one thing, and then you hit him with something else. It's not rocket science. Basically, you can be successful … I had a 28-year successful kickboxing career. That's pretty much the basics. I worked defense first, which was different. Most guys don't. They get in the gym, they're all about, "What am I going to hit today?" They're not about getting in the ring to start moving.

I watched Duran. Duran thinks more like me as well. Well, at least when I saw him training for Leonard, the first fight. He was in Miami. He was doing the … moving around the ring for 20 minutes warming up, just slipping punches, not even really worried about throwing. He was just moving, bobbing and weaving. Man, when I looked at him, I thought, "Wow, if he decides he doesn't want to get hit by Leonard, he's not going get hit because he just looks so great defensively." Think about it, this is a guy like Duran, who's a great fighter, real experienced, and yet these young amateurs come in there and they don't do five minutes of warm-up like that. They don't want to spend time in the rain. They just want to get their gloves on and start punching the bag.

JL: Fundamentals.

DW: Fundamentals, so those are the two things you know.

JL: I've got one more question for you. Instead of the other question, which was what would tell you, this is what would you tell our audience today? We've got people from all over the world. They train in different ways for different reasons. What would you leave to them with today?

DW: You know what I'd like to say to your audience, anybody who sees this? I have had, in my life, two careers – one was a pro fighter, and one was a pro actor. Neither career would have been successful if it wasn't for the audience, because nobody makes money as a fighter if you don't have the stands full of people. Nobody makes money as an actor if people are not watching it, if the Nielsen ratings aren't high, or because it wasn't theatrical for me, or if they are not renting the videos or not buying the DVDs.

The only way that I was able to have fun I had, because it was really a lot of fun being a kickboxer, and the successful secondary career that Chuck Norris suggested that I do, the acting, is because of the audience. It's because of them, directly as a result of their support. I was able to have people tell me, "Don, you're the luckiest guy in the world. You're the luckiest kickboxer ever. You're the luckiest actor." Actors don't come out here and then two years later star on HBO, because it doesn't happen. Millions of people come every year to be actors, and it doesn't happen. They don't get to be stars in movies that often. How many kickboxers can you say starred in 30 films?

JL: Other than you, none.

DW: Not Hong Kong films. I'm talking about Hollywood films. I'm it. A lot of people thought, "Oh you're a world-champion kickboxer. That's why you starred in all these movies," and I said no. It maybe got my break in the beginning, but it wasn't that. It was that I have support from millions of people all over the world who supported my movies, supported my fight career, and I'd like to say thank you to all of them because that's how … The last thing, the ending of the interview is thank you to all the fans.

JL: What a great conversation. I want to thank Don for coming on, for being so open, and honest, and fun. Sometimes we get big names on the show and I get a little bit nervous they're not going to be fun, but guess what? They've all been super fun. There's something that I think that says about martial arts and what we do. The fact that the biggest names in our space are some of the kindest, friendliest, most entertaining people that you could imagine. I am glad we were able to bring this episode to you, and I wanted to shout out Andrew for all of his hard work in making this one happen. It's not always easy to get big names.

For listeners, if you appreciate this episode, if you appreciate the other things that we do, please consider supporting us, whether it be on Patreon, whether it be with reviews or purchases, books, or whatever it is, please consider. To those of you who already do, thank you. You know how much I appreciate you.

If you have topic or guest suggestions, don't be afraid to reach out. My email: Jeremy@whistlekick.com. Our social media is @whistlekick, and that brings us to the end.

Until next time, train hard, smile, and have a great day.

GRANDMASTER CYNTHIA ROTHROCK

"We did a movie together (Fight to Win-1987), and have done lots of seminars together. A wonderful woman and a great technician."

— Bill Wallace

"She is very friendly with me and always comes to support me when I ask her."

— Fumio Demura

"Cynthia Rothrock has always been the consummate professional martial artist. Always kind and attentive to everyone. A class act all the way and I am proud to know her."

—Jeff Speakman

Jeremy Lesniak: What's up, everybody? Welcome. This is whistlekick Martial Arts Radio, episode 640. My guest today, Cynthia Rothrock.

I'm Jeremy Lesniak. I'm your host here for the show and founder of whistlekick. What do we do at whistlekick? Well, we do a whole bunch of stuff for people probably like you, people who love the traditional martial arts. If you want to see what that means, all the stuff we've got going on, go to whistlekick.com. You're going to find a lot of stuff over there: our projects, our products, and one of the ways that we pay the bills for all this stuff is our store. You might find something in there that you like, whether it's a T-shirt, or sweatshirt, maybe some protective gear, we've got uniforms, we've got a bunch of different stuff. It's constantly changing.

Now, if you want to go deeper on this or any other episode, go to whistlekickmartialartsradio.com. You're going to find a separate page over there for each and every episode we have ever done. None of this is behind a paywall. You're going to find, on each of those pages, transcripts, and links, and photos, and videos, and whatever else is going to give you more context for the show.

Now, if you like what we do, if it means something to you, consider supporting us in some way, whether that's telling friends about what we do, or checking out one of the things you can buy, like some gear or a shirt, or one of our books on Amazon, or we've also got a Patreon, patreon.com/whistlekick. If you like what we do, you're probably going to like what we do at Patreon, because we do other stuff, exclusive stuff, stuff you're not going to find anywhere else, behind the scenes on this show, and so much more. It starts at two bucks a month, and the more you're willing to plunk down, the more we're going to give you, so check it out.

For many of you out there, today's guest needs no introduction. With over 60 movies under her belt, a competitive career that few – if anyone, honestly – have ever achieved, and recognition in the arts for being just an incredible practitioner. Grandmaster Cynthia Rothrock is someone that I've been looking forward to having on the show for a very long time. I could say more, but I'm not going to. Here's our conversation.

First off, thanks for doing this. Thanks for coming on.

Cynthia Rothrock: Oh, well, thanks for bearing with me with all my trials and tribulations going on here.

JL: Of course. Yeah, you've had some stuff going on.

CR: Oh, man, I know. Always, right? It's always something.

JL: There is always something and that's ... but isn't that part of what martial arts conditions us for? It gives us that toolbox to reach into and persist?

CR: Yep, absolutely. It gets stronger and stronger, no matter what. You've got to keep going, no matter what.

JL: Yes. That's right. We got to keep going.

CR: Yeah.

JL: Well, then we're going to play from moment zero for the audience.

CR: Okay.

JL: We don't need to edit. We're just going to do it. We're going to do.

CR: Okay!

JL: Now, we're eventually going to deviate off, but I like to have a little bit of context to launch from. For me as an interviewer, this is my launch pad.

CR: Sure.

JL: It's a question I'm sure you've answered a whole bunch of times, and I promise it's going to start to shift and meld from there, so let's just get that one out of the way, and that is, how did you get started?

CR: Well, I got started when I was 13 years old, and my girlfriend's parents were studying Tang Soo Do at the Scranton Karate School, and they owned a health club. We would go down on Sunday when the club was closed, and my friend and I would do cartwheels, and rolls, and try to play out in the big open carpet area. Then, they would come and start practicing their techniques, and I was infatuated with it. Like, what is that? I'd never seen anything like it, never saw the uniforms. I thought, "Oh, my gosh, learning how to defend yourself with your hands and feet?" I said, "I want to try that," so I went home and told my mom. I said, "I want to sign up in karate."

JL: What did she say, because that … Back then – and I don't want to put too fine a point on any of this – very few people were training, and the perception, at least from my understanding, was that it wasn't always well received.

CR: Well, back then, there weren't too many schools. It was one of the few. Nobody really knew what it was. It was a fallacy that you had to be a big, strong man to take karate. My mom had no idea what it was. She was used to me … I've always been kind of an out-of-the-box kind of person. Anything that was unusual or different, that's what I wanted to do, and this to me was really unusual.

I did a lot of things. I did baton, I did music, I did dance, I did different musical instruments, and my mom was just used to me trying all these different things. When we went in to sign up, I had to sign up for four months, so my mom was like, "Okay, you're committed for four months," because she was used to me going, "Oh, yeah, I'll try it. I don't like it. Okay, I don't like it. I don't like it." I remember taking guitar lessons at a young age and my fingers were being so … they were so sore that I couldn't even press in the … you know, with calluses, and they were bleeding just pressing in on the strings, so my mom was used to me doing all kinds of crazy things, and she just said, "Okay, we could try it."

JL: Over the years of doing this show, I've found that the guests generally have a pretty solid memory for their initial entrance into martial arts, so let's test if that holds true for you here. Were you at all intimidated about this four-month commitment? Were you going into it thinking, "If I don't like it, I'll just wander away, and I'll deal with that with my mother later," or was there something about it, you said, "You know, this feels different?"

CR: I was excited to do something different. When I went in there, my friend's parents were not in the class, so I didn't know anybody. I'm a young girl, and there's all men in the class. They had one woman there that was a black belt, and she was there, and she didn't really like another woman being in the class. She tried to scare me. I remember on my second class, my instructor paired me up to spar with her. I had no idea how to spar. It was my second class! She hit me in the head with a roundhouse kick, almost knocked me out. I was like, "Oh, gosh, I don't know if I like this." My instructor called me in the office, and he says, "Yeah, you don't block with your head."

Then on my next class, someone tried to have me break a board with a front kick because I just learned how to do a front kick. I didn't know how to pull my toes back. Well, of course, I hit, and it was a small board, too. It was one that was already broken, and you know that's much harder to break than a full board. I thought I broke my toe.

Then again, we were doing push-ups and shouting, and I was very intimidated. I was intimidated, and I did not want to continue. I went home and I told my mom, I said, "I don't like this." There was nothing good about it at the time. I just kept getting hurt and hurt and hurt. My mother said, "You know what, I have to pay for four months, you're going," so I went. My mom would take me. It was like the old scenario where the parents dragged them off to music lessons or dance lessons.

It was about two months into training, and we were sitting there, and we were getting ready. We had stripes then, and I was going for my black belt stripe. You didn't have to test, but it was like an achievement thing, a morale boost for you. My instructor gave a talk, and he said, "Losers are quitters, and if you're not good, it's your fault because you have a bad attitude, and you have to change your attitude." He just gave this talk that I felt was directly to me. I thought, "You know what?" I could never get that form, basic one, I couldn't get that turn, and I said, "You know? I have a bad attitude. I hate push-ups. I'm intimidated in this class. It's all men." I said, "You know, I have to do it for four months, so you know what?" I was embarrassed at this talk, although he never mentioned my name, but I just felt it was dear to me. I said, "I'm going to start practicing. I'm going to change my attitude."

I started thinking, yeah, I hate push-ups, but you know what? They're really good for my body, and they're really going to make me stronger. Then, I started getting better, and I kept practicing that move in basic one, and finally, I got it. Then I started saying, "Hey, I could shout in class." I was afraid to shout, this little girl with all these guys shouting. I just built up my confidence. It's a lesson that I have learned for the rest of my life, from that moment, is that you don't give up because things are hard. You know? I thank my mom, because you know how you always say, "If it wasn't for my parents, I wouldn't be where I am today." Well, that's true, because being a young girl, and so intimidated, I would have quit.

JL: That moment, that speech from your instructor, it sounds pretty pivotal, and one of those moments that I would imagine on your martial arts journey we could put a pin in and say this is a marked transition between where you were and where you went.

There's another piece in there, and that's you having the ability, the consciousness, to receive that speech in the right way. Where did that come from? As a 13-year-old girl, what you're describing doesn't sound typical. I've known 13-year-old girls. I've known a number of them in various contexts, and I don't think any of them would have heard that speech and said, "You know what? I'm all in."

CR: I know. It just sunk into my mind, you know? I think that … I'm a strong believer in faith, and I think that … Well, I don't think, I know that martial arts has been my life's journey, and I'm doing what I'm supposed to do, and I think it just clicked into me. When I was five and a half months training, I was already an orange belt, and I skipped. I went from orange belt to orange belt - one stripe, which was unheard of at that time, to skip a stripe. Because of that, when I started feeling I was getting better, it fired my training to keep going, and I am going to get good at this, and I really love this, and I love push-ups now.

I entered a competition. At that time … We're talking about like the late 70s … mid 70s, actually, and we're talking about at competition, it was just "Women." They didn't have any, so if you were a white belt, or if you were a grandmaster, you are in one division – "Women." I took second place. A black belt took first, and actually, the black belt from my school that hit me in the head took third. I took second, and I was like, "Oh my gosh, I'm only an orange belt. I've only been training for five and a half months, and I beat black belts." That fired me up to say, "You know what? I am going to train because I want to be the best in martial arts, and I can do this." From that day on, I went from two times a week to going four times a week, and training with a passion, with a fury, that, "I am going to excel in this martial arts."

JL: Any fallout from beating your … let's call her your rival?

CR: Well, yes, because I did not spar her, until I was a red belt, again. My instructor never had me spar her, and let's just say payback time.

JL: I like it. I'm guessing there's no video of this, is there?

CR: No. I mean, I wish because back then, everybody … we had like this … the Super Eight cameras, where you have the film and stuff like that wasn't easy, like the way you have your phones today, but I wish. I have pictures. I have pictures of training. I remember … We're talking about old school training. We're not talking about today, where instructors are really watching out for the students. We're talking about an era that if you couldn't hang in there, you were out of there. They didn't care. It wasn't a business. It was like the instructors were doing this part time and it was all about, "If you can't hang with us, you're out." I remember when I was getting ready to test for my black belt, they brought three Koreans over from Korea. They came into our school for three weeks and they said, "Yeah, your students are good, but they don't know how to fight."

For three weeks, fighting every single day, and this was brutal. This is like throw a spinning wheel kick and you knew your other leg was getting knocked out. I would go home with bruises, and I couldn't walk, and I was limping. My mom was like, "You need to quit." I'm like, "No, no, no!" I remember my instructor told me that if they didn't like someone in the school, they would beat them up so they would quit. I was like, "Are you trying to make me quit?" He's like, "No, no, no," but lesson learned. From that day on … I used to spar at that time in competition. I was never afraid to spar another woman again, because I knew that they were not going to hurt me and hit me as hard as the Koreans did, because they didn't care if you were a young girl or whatever, you were going to be a good fighter.

JL: Wow. We have almost this complete 180 with this other woman who tried to kick you out, tried to push you away. I would imagine that, especially at that age, you felt that the weight of that was on you. Then you go ahead and you defeat her in competition, and then you go on to exact your revenge. We can look at that in the playful way that it is, but at the same time, there's some pretty substantial growth, personal growth, in facing that obstacle which happened to be that person and overcoming it, and some of the words you're choosing tell me that was another really pivotal moment in your training.

CR: Oh, absolutely. After I became a black belt, I started teaching, and you just realize that if you're a black belt and you're sparring a white belt for their second class, there's no way you're going to hit them in the head. You just don't do that. You should have the control, you should have the respect. I guess I think that's what always was in my head is that I had no clue what I was doing, and that was totally uncalled for, because to me, if you're a black belt, you have to have control and focus, and you do not hit your beginning students in the head.

JL: It's a bad business model, if nothing else.

CR: Well, it almost worked because I almost quit.

JL: Let's talk about competition a little further, though. A lot of the folks who are listening right now know you from your competitive career, which I believe is the launch pad, but the way you talked about competition and getting into competition, take us back. What was that first event like? Were you excited, nervous, something else, more than one? Take us through that journey?

CR: Well, I was always nervous, even when I was competing professionally, and I was undefeated five years. I was always nervous before I competed. I would go there, and I wouldn't be able to eat, and I'd be running the bathroom 100 times, and I couldn't talk to anybody, and I would constantly be going over my forms and my weapons in my head, over and over and over.

The night before I would compete, I would have … I thought my routine was to have a big pasta meal, lots of carbs, and go to bed thinking of your form. Then, the minute I got on the floor to start, everything went away, all the nerves went away, the confidence went away, and it was a different thing, but I've always gotten nervous. a lot of people say to me, "You know, I get nervous." I'll say, "Yeah, that's kind of good, because it builds up your adrenaline and it just makes you stronger." I've never lost that to any competition, of never feeling nervous before.

When I won that, I started going to a lot of competitions. I remember fighting black belt for the first time. I was lightweight, and then they had a heavyweight. Everybody was saying she was going to kill me, and they were scaring me. I was so nervous. I remember I was in the bathroom and so nervous again, because I'm in the Grand Champion finals fighting, first-time black belt. I heard these girls saying, "Oh, yeah," and the girl's name was Pearl. "Pearl's gonna kill her. Oh my God."

I'm like, "UGH," but what happened is they got my adrenaline up so much, and we go to spar, and within three seconds, she hits me in the face with a backfist. Now at this time, we didn't have safety equipment, and it was contact, not full contact, but you had to make pretty hard contact to get a point. I got embarrassed. I was like, "Oh my gosh, it was like only three seconds, she got me."

Then, all of a sudden, something came over me. I remember I just got this fury, and I was throwing my kicks at her, and I ended up winning the match against Pearl, but I got so confident that I remember I even did a jumping front kick, and I'm like, "Who does a jumping front kick when they're sparring?"

That was competition for me, and I just competed everywhere, in the Eastern Region 10 states for Karate Illustrated. I became number one in that area. Then I went to a tournament New Jersey. It was an A-rated tournament, and it was actually held at the Playboy Club or something. It was the Playboy Club tournament, but it was an A-rated tournament, and I took first place there. Everybody was coming up to me going, "Who are you? Oh my God, you beat the woman that's number one, and you need to compete professionally."

I met George Chung there, and Ernie Reyes, the West Coast Demonstration Team, and they invited me to go out to California and compete out there. Because of them and their inspiration, I ended up moving to California, competing in all the professional competitions for five years, because that was my goal. I wanted to be undefeated for five years – and that's competing in over 100 tournaments, that's not just five times – and then retire. I set that goal, and I made it. The last tournament I did was in 1985, the Bermuda Internationals. I won that, and then at the same time, I got an offer to do a movie, so my career shifted. It went from being a martial art instructor, to a competitor, to now going into movies, so I just feel like I was on the right path, the way my life was supposed to be, to help people, to inspire people, and to be the best that I could be.

JL: We're definitely going to talk about the movies because just as I know a lot of people listening know you from competition, even more know you from your time on screen, but I want to unpack that goal, 100 competitions.

CR: Yeah, so it's [inaudible 20:32] undefeated …

JL: Five years, undefeated? What?!

CR: Yeah, and it's embarrassing to say that.

JL: That's a big goal!

CR: It is! It was a big goal.

JL: People today … Not everyone follows a circuit with points, so people may not remember what that was like. I started doing competitions in the 90s. I was chasing points, and one could suffer a loss, you could get second, you could get third, and still be way out in front in rankings, but that's not what your goal was. Your goal wasn't, "I'm going to be ranked first for five years." It was I'm going to go undefeated. We're talking about forms?

CR: Yes, we're talking about forms.

JL: Okay, forms, undefeated, five years, 100-ish competitions. That's a big reach. Now, obviously, you did it, so you weren't reaching too far, but I think there's a lot … there's something in here for all of us, if you can dig into the where and why that goal came from.

CR: Well, I'll tell you what, it was hard. It was a very challenging goal for me, because for those five years, all I did is train and train. I would train at least eight hours a day. I would win a competition, I would come back and continue training. I went to mainland China and studied in Chengdu in 1982, when Americans had a really hard time to get into China.

I remember training in Chengdu, and I would attract crowds, because they've never seen blue eyes in there. Then my friend, who was African American, they never saw an African American. We would attract these people because we were like aliens coming from another planet because China was not open to people then. I went there and studied for eight weeks. I studied in Taiwan, I studied in Hong Kong prior.

I just kept going, "I have to be better, I have to be better, I have to be better." I know some people would … they'd win their division, and they'd go, "Okay, I could rest now," but I wouldn't. I would just go train harder.

The more I went as the years went by, the more pressure it became because everybody was trying to beat Cynthia Rothrock. It got to the point, after three years, I'm like, "Oh my gosh, if I got beat, that would be embarrassing for me because it would be big news," so I kept making my routines more difficult and harder. Then the harder they got, it was like something … It doesn't matter how good you are. If you're doing this extreme balanced movement … and I don't know if you remember, but back in the day, they had tarps on the floors for this event, that if you're on a big wrinkle on the tarp, you could lose your balance, so it was a big pressure for me.

I had a love/hate when I retired. I wanted to keep going, but also, I was glad that I did this, and now it's time to move on, to go, but I tell you, when you put a goal like that … I didn't do anything else. I did some ballet. I did gymnastics. I did anything that I felt would help my martial arts, but I wouldn't go skiing. I wouldn't go hiking. I wouldn't tour. If I went to a city, I was looking for a martial arts school to train. I literally could say for those five years, I ate, drank and slept martial arts.

JL: Is the word "obsessed" a fair word?

CR: I wouldn't say it's obsessed. I think it was determination.

JL: Okay.

CR: It was determination to get that goal that I achieved for myself, and that I was working so hard at. It was my love. Martial arts was my love. I love training. I love practicing. I love getting stronger. I love getting faster. I loved challenging myself and more difficult movements. I wouldn't say it's obsessed. I would just say it was my passion.

JL: Passion, determination. Anyone who's ever set a lofty goal and achieved it knows that you have to do that. You can't set a big goal and just sit on your butt and expect it to happen. It doesn't work that way.

CR: Yeah, absolutely.

JL: You talked a little bit about the things that you didn't do. What I'm curious about is how this approach to this goal, this passion and determination, were received by … you talked about your mom and her varied perspective on your training, initially for, maybe a little less so once it got a little rougher, but you talked about some of these people who were your inspiration, your motivation. You didn't use those words, I am, but what did these people around you think of your drive?

CR: Hmm, that's a good question. My parents were very proud. I remember when I brought my first trophy home. My mom was so proud, and then there was 10, and then there was 20, and now there's 100, and now they're moved up into the attic. Just recently, I had to go back to my mom's, because my mom passed away, and I had to go back and clear out the trophies.

JL: Oh, I'm sorry.

CR: I had over 1,000 trophies in my mom's shed that's been there since the 70s, because this is all prior to me moving to California in 1981. I moved to California then, and I didn't come back. I stayed there. I think they were very … well, I know, I don't think, they were extremely proud of me.

I remember when I was on the cover of Karate Illustrated, that was a big step because Renardo Barton was the editor, and he wanted to put me on, and he was told that women do not sell as the complete cover. He fought, and fought, and fought for me, and I got on the cover. I remember my dad going down to the local magazine store and buying them out, and he's going, "This is my daughter." They're like, "No, it isn't," and he's like, "Yes! It is! It is!"

They actually never really saw me compete because when I was competing locally, I would just go and do it myself. Then, when I was doing all the professional ones, my dad did come to one professional tournament, and it was in New Jersey. He was so excited to be there, and I was so excited that my dad was going to be there, and the guy was a crook. The guy ran off with all the money, and there was no tournament unfortunately.

JL: Oh, no!

CR: Oh, my gosh. Yeah, so it was crazy. They never got to see me really compete.

JL: Wow. Okay. Now, the step into movies, it sounds like that was pretty quickly after this five-year run. Was that something you had your eye on?

CR: No, it wasn't. I'll tell you, I started training with Sheum Leung in New York City. Every Sunday, I would go drive three hours to New York, train all day, then my teacher would take us to Chinatown and go see a Hong Kong movie, and have dinner, and then I would drive back. Every Sunday I did that, for years and years. Well, then I became accustomed to Hong Kong movies, and I loved Jackie Chan. I would come home and I would practice the movements that I'd seen Jackie Chan doing, like in *Snake and the Eagle's Shadow* and all this, and I loved the fact that he would take implements, like a telephone, and use it as a whip, and I would just practice that. I just loved the movies, but I never really thought I would be in movies, and I never really had an aspiration to be an actor. I just loved them.

Then, when I moved to the west coast, I was on the West Coast Demonstration Team, and we performed at every competition, and it was one of the first, I think, actually, that I know of, demonstration teams. Ernie Reyes brought it out with music, and laughter, and everybody on the team was excellent. Well, Paul Maslak was the editor of Inside Kung Fu, and he hears that Corey Yuen, famous Hong Kong director, is coming to audition for a new Bruce Lee, they were looking for a guy to be the next Bruce Lee. He called Ernie Reyes in Georgetown, and he said, "Well, yeah, we'll bring the guys. What about the girls?" They said, "Yeah, yeah, you can bring them, but you know, we're really looking for a guy."

We all went down to Los Angeles, and I remember it was at [29:06 Heyul Cho's] studio and there were 1,000 martial artists there. Now it's my turn and Corey Yuen was there, and I had to do some form, I did some self-defense, I did some free sparring, and I did my double hook sword form in my weapons. I remember hooking the two hooks together, and [29:27 Heyul Cho's] studio was low on the ceiling, and I remember my hooks hit the ceiling and all this plaster was coming down on top of me. I'm thinking, "Oh, my gosh."

Well, then Corey Yuen goes back to Seasonal Films, who he was casting for, and he says, "I want the girl. I want the girl. I don't want a guy," and that's how it started. They cast me into it. I always … I learned a lesson from that, too, that I tell my people, is that sometimes, if you want to do film or whatever, and they're looking for someone else, but you go in there and you do your best, you can change their minds.

It brings me … My daughter, when she was four, they were doing a play at her school, and it was *Alice in Wonderland.* She was very talented, even at that young age, and her acting teachers wanted her to go out for Alice, and she said, "No, I want to be the Queen of Hearts." They're like, "Cynthia, you know, she'd be great for Alice, but the Queen of Hearts, you know, is like, for an eighth grader." She said, "No, I'm going to do it." She went out, and I tried to … I was thinking of it, and I said, "Okay," and I was trying to do like the Austin Powers … the Mini-Me thing, and I was trying to get her to put the little finger by her mouth.

She has no clue who Austin Powers is, but anyway, she goes in, and she just kicks it out of the ballpark, and they ended up casting her as the Mini-Me Queen that mocked the Queen of Hearts. If it wasn't for her determination, she would not have got the part she wanted, but that's what she wanted to do and loved it. You can change people's perceptions if you're in the acting. Just go in with confidence and faith and do your best.

JL: Those early days acting … You talked about how on the competition floor, you never shed the nerves of getting out there. Different when you were on the floor, which I can actually relate to completely, but that lead up to it, was it the same thing with movies? Were you nervous running choreography and lines, but once the cameras were on, it all fell away?

CR: Not once I started. Before, I did the movie, I was nervous. Here I am. I'm on a plane. I'm going to Hong Kong. I'm doing a movie. All I know is Chinese movies. I'm thinking they're going to have me dressed in a Chinese outfit, I'm going to have black braids with razor blades in, I'm going to be spinning my head around, I'm going to Han's Island from *Enter the Dragon*, you know? I have no clue what to expect. I know nobody there. I'm on myself. Never did a movie, right? I get out there, and they go, "Oh," and nobody really spoke English except the one producer, Amy Chow, who is Raymond Chow's daughter. She goes "No, you're going to play Cindy, a cop from England," and I was like, "Oh, I am?" I was extremely nervous before I shot because I'd never shot, I didn't know the people, but you know, I think it's still like that. If I'm doing a new movie, I'm always nervous on the first day. Then, once you get in there, and you get the jitters out, and then you get calm, then I was good the next … from that point on. It's funny, always, at first, I'd still get that nervousness, whether it was competition or starting a new movie on the first day of shooting.

JL: You're nervous about things you care about it. I've coached a number of competitors over the years, and they'll come to me, "Jeremy, I'm really nervous." Well, that shows what you're about to do matters to you. If you weren't nervous, then I would wonder if you actually cared.

CR: Yeah, that's a good point. Trust me, I would love to have not been nervous, but it's just how it goes, how my system and my body worked.

JL: What was the rest of that experience of that first film like? Clearly, coming out of it you enjoyed it well enough, because you went on to do a few more.

CR: Yeah, yeah. It was tough. It was really tough. Corey Yuen put Michelle Yeoh and I, our first movie, *Yes, Madam!*, through the ringer, and I didn't know anything about filming, so I had short sleeves on, and I was beat up. I remember there was one scene that both of us were so black and blue he had to cut it out because we were flinching every time someone would hit us. It was a movie that was supposed to be four months. It went eight and a half months. I was eight and a half months in Hong Kong. Just the ending fight scene was … took one month to do it, and it was dangerous. It was hard, but I just said, "You know what? I'm going to try my best and do what I can do, and I'm not going to be afraid, and I'm going to challenge myself."

I think that's, even today … I still do movies here and there and stuff, but I got into extreme adventure, where I have trekked to Everest Base Camp, I did Inca Trail, I did Patagonia, the W Trek. I like to challenge myself physically, and that's how my new challenge has gone into extreme adventures. I think …

JL: I didn't know this. I didn't know about this with you.

CR: Oh, yeah!

JL: When did this start?

CR: Oh, I think this started … Well, let's see. I had my daughter in 1999, and we started traveling places together. Then she became … sixth grade, 12-ish. She didn't want to travel with mom anymore. I enjoyed traveling, I enjoyed doing all the adventures, so I started booking adventure trips, and I went to New Zealand for one month, and I did the most extreme whitewater rafting, the highest commercial waterfall you could go down. My fear was I was going to tip over, and that's exactly what happened, tipped over under the falls, but again, I was glad I did that because I realized that, hey, there's some air underneath the raft, and all you have to do is get out of the rushing water, put your head underneath it, and go, and you'll be fine. The idea is not to panic.

From that point on, I was doing one a year, to two a year, to three a year, and even now, I was supposed to trek the Alps from all across Italy on September 3. Unfortunately, I got pneumonia, bacterial pneumonia, from who knows where, from one of my travels or just coming back from an event where there were a lot of people, and I had to cancel it. I'm disappointed, but I will do that.

Also, when COVID happened, I didn't work for a year and a half, and I'm used to being … traveling more than I'm home, whether it's for work or adventure, and I started scuba diving. I said, "you know what, I can do that here. It's not around a lot of people. I have found that is another passion of mine, and I got certified in December. Right now, I have 103 dives. I find that when I find something I really like, I just seek it, with a passion. That's what I love doing now, and hopefully I get back … I teach seminars around the world, and that's another thing I love. I love teaching, and a lot of times people … If they don't know me, they just know me as an actor, they don't know that, yes, I'm an eighth-degree black belt, and I love teaching. They'll go, "Oh my God, wow, she's can really teach." I'm like, "Uh, yeah."

That's kind of what I'm doing now.

JL: If we had to draw a line between martial arts training, and movies, and the adventures, the obvious connection is challenge, but one could make the argument that you've been training long enough that the challenge is a little different now. You have to invent, I would imagine, your own challenges to stay challenged with the movies. You've done enough of them that if you're going to be challenged in a movie, it's because you're picking a role that maybe isn't quite what you've done before. The adventures … Now, the reason I'm structuring this very complex question is because I think there's something underneath here, and I want to take away that easy answer of, "Oh, they're all challenging." What do they have in common? What is it about you that these are things that you gravitate towards?

CR: You know? That's a good question. I think I like overcoming obstacles, because I have a fear of heights, but yet I bungee, I skydive, I went very high off of a raft over rapids. I think I like the adrenaline rush. Like in competition, I had that adrenaline rush before. Adventure. Movies … I think when I do movies … Movies, I love doing. It's a fun job for me. I guess a lot of the film roles I've done haven't been challenging. Some of the were, which I love, when I played, like in *Sworn to Justice*, a psychologist, and I had to learn all these different terms, or *Santa's Summer House* and I played Mrs. Claus. I love that, but a lot of the films were just Cynthia Rothrock, girl next door, the cop, fight through this and that, so that just was up my alley.

I think the more challenging thing was more in the competition. Not only just the competition, it was weapons. I loved weapons. I wanted to do … I remember doing the double steel whips, and getting them tangled, and getting hit in the head with a spear, or doing my three sectional staff and conking myself in the shins. Many times, my weapon of competition was the hook swords. Just walking into a competition with my hook swords, and having them down by my side, and the hook blade that was so sharp hitting my pants and cutting me, blood running down my legs.

I think I'm just … I'm a different person. I seek challenge, and I seek adventure. It's not that I just challenge myself. I love it. I love being in nature. I love that. When I'm hiking, I'm at peace. When I'm under the water scuba diving, I'm in a different world, like, "Oh, my gosh, look at this world that's so different, that I never would have known existed." I wouldn't have known that these different, awesome marine life existed.

I think, if I had to say, it's just my thirst for life, just to do the things I really like to do. I'm at a stage now where I love doing movies, I've done over 60, and I'd love to continue doing them, but right now, I feel like I really want to give back to people. I think we get, in life, where it's, "Us, us, us, focus, focus, focus," and now I'm trying to do things, humanitarian, not trying to … One of the things I tried to do, I'm very popular on Facebook, and I talk to everybody, and I have a lot of followers, and I just try to be positive and uplift people. I get a lot of people that will message me that they're depressed or this and that, and I feel like I can help people out that way.

When I was doing martial arts movies, I felt that too, because I remember women would say, "Oh, my gosh, I …" and men, too. Men, not just women. "I started martial arts because I saw you doing films," and that, to me, is something that I think makes it all worth it, that I got – through movies or through seeing me in competition or whatever – brought people into martial arts, because I really do have a passion that everyone should learn some type of martial arts. Not if you want to compete or do movies or whatever, but it's just, to me, the best thing in the world a person can do for themselves. Gets you in great shape, but at the same time, you can defend yourself, and maybe you could defend someone else, and if that happens, that's priceless.

JL: I couldn't agree more. Now, the dots that you laid out, I want to connect them. I want to guess something about you. This didn't come through in your words, but it's what I'm taking from it. When someone tells you, you can't do something, what's your response?

CR: I'll do it.

JL: Yeah, that's … See, and that was my guess. What I heard out of those things, out of the stories you've given, is a very quiet rebelliousness.

CR: Yeah, I think so. I think I'm such an adamant person and about people … about age, like, "Oh, age, oh, this," and to me, that's not in my vocabulary. When I was trekking up to Everest, about the third day, my knee blew out and I couldn't even walk. Luckily, I met this amazing doctor there that did acupuncture, and I was able to do everything on sticks, but my guide said to my friend that was doing the trip with me, "Oh, she might have to go back." He said, "If I know her, she'll crawl up the mountain if she has to," and that's my attitude. I remember, I was in [44:01 Cave Verdo] with my friend Vincent [44:03 Lan], and we were on these high cliffs, and he jumped in, and I had a dress on. He's like, "Come on in," and remember again, I have that fear of heights, and I have a dress on, and I was like, "Oh," I didn't want to get all wet, my hair and makeup are going to do all this stuff, but he dared me then. Then, I said, "Oh, you dare me?" Then I jumped in. I think, yeah, I don't like it if people say you can't do something. I really don't, because …

JL: I had a feeling.

CR: Yeah. There's a difference. Do you want to, or just say you can't. I think anybody could do anything to the best of their abilities if you put your mind to it.

JL: I agree. Where else has that … let's call it rebellious. This is called what it is. Where else has that surfaced, and has it ever backfired? Has it bit you?

CR: Has it bit me? I'm sure, probably. I can't think of it right now, but I'm sure it has. Life is not like, what is the saying, a bowl of cherries? Everybody has their ups and downs, and everybody has stress, and everybody has bad things happen in their life. It's just how we deal with it. I try to stay pretty positive. I try not to let negative influences or … you get haters out there, but once in a while, I'll go off on someone, I have a couple pet peeves, like if someone challenges my martial art ability, I have to say something, you know?

JL: Can we unpack that? Let me set why, because this is not a subject we generally get into. We're in a very weird time, martial arts-wise, because we are so connected, and that with the layer, this tone that's come out of cancel culture, people look for everything they can tear each other apart for. Let's face it, as martial artists, we were known for doing that to each other already, and it's gotten really bad. As a public figure, one of the probably best-known martial artists in the West for sure, I would imagine you attract a lot of that. Yeah, you can point at your competitive career, you can point at your movies, you have all kinds of things you can point to and say, "Yeah, I've done my thing. I know what I'm doing," and you could just ignore it all, but it gets you riled up, probably in a similar way that it gets me riled up. Could you talk about why and how you address it, and how you reconcile that with the staying positive that you feel strongly about?

CR: Right. I think in general, most people are pretty positive, but you do have people out there that live in negativity, whether they're unhappy with their life, or they're jealous of other people's happiness or positivity, and they just come after you. I just try to say, "Why are you living in negativity? It's got to make you feel worse," or whatever. Usually what happens is I will kind of shame them in a way, and then they come back … Either they go away, or they say, "Oh, well, I'm sorry, I just did it …" Whatever, but I try not to get into that, because like I said, I don't like negative, but sometimes you just get pulled into it. A lot of times people will say something, and I'll be like, "Who? Who are they talking about?" They're like, "You." I'm like, "Me? What? Me? What? Why me? Who doesn't like me?"

I really feel like I'm … People that have said bad things about me or whatever, because of their whatever reasons, when I see them, I'm still nice, "Hey, how you doing?" or whatever. I just like … You don't have time for all that, but it happens to everybody, not just me. It happens, it happens. I see it. To all my friends, it happens to everybody that … There's just some people out there that go after you.

JL: You've mentioned your friends. You've named dropped some pretty big names in the martial arts. You've, I would imagine, met, worked with, trained with, pretty much anybody that we could mention, so instead of spending the next 10 minutes on a list, are there any stories that are favorites of yours that you might be willing to share?

CR: Like what? Like stories of … I have lots of stories!

JL: Oh, I know! You know what? The stories that our audience seems to appreciate the most aren't the ones that are the big, and the flashy, and the dramatic. It's the ones that mean a lot to whoever's presenting them, so a moment, it could be a moment, it could be a meal, it could be something with hopefully somebody that many of us have heard of that we wouldn't have heard that story before, kind of a behind the scenes in the life of Cynthia Rothrock.

CR: I've had so many near-death situations filming in Hong Kong that it got to where …

JL: Wait, what?!

CR: Yeah … like where I thought I was going to get killed, like from doing extremely dangerous stunts and doing them. I remember, every time there was one, and then they'd just up it the next time, and I'd go, "Oh, I think this is going to be my last one." Then I do the movie and … I got hurt on every one, just like Jackie Chan. That's just how Hong Kong filming is, but then you'd heal, and you'd see the film, and you'd be, "Oh, my God. When's my next one?"

I have a lot that kind of stories, but I think one that I'm really proud of is that Arnold Schwarzenegger and Dr. Bob Goldman have the International Sports Hall of Fame, which is football players, A-listed actors, top bodybuilders, the top of the top, whether it's track, Olympians, and I think it was in 2014, I was the first person … martial artist, male or female, inducted into the International Sports Hall of Fame. I was very honored. I'm in a lot of Hall of Fames, and they all mean a lot to me, but this one was particular because I felt like, "Wow, I am representing everybody in martial arts, not just the women." The very first person to be inducted into the probably most prestigious Hall of Fame, like Black Belt Hall of Fame, to do that.

That was a memory point that I always cherish, not so much for me, but just for … I like to uplift women, too. Overcoming the problems that women have, like getting involved in action film, or, like I said, being on the cover of a magazine, or whatever. I just, throughout my whole life, when I first started doing some of my movies in the US, I was always the partner, and then the guy had to come in and save the day, because like, "Oh, no, no, no, the woman can't do that," but changing the world, changing the perception of powerful, strong women, that's … A lot that I try to do right now is try to uplift women.

JL: Is that changing? I know it's changed for you personally, but for women in the industry, is it changing?

CR: I think it's changing. Definitely, more women are getting involved. More women are … To me, because I came up in an industry that was male-dominated, I never trained or felt like, "Oh, I'm the woman, take care of me," this and that. I always felt as an equal, and I think women are feeling that right now. There's so many more women involved in martial arts, and stunts, and acting that it is changing.

There's still things that you deal with, like, right now, I remember … Remember I told you I have this age thing? I'm an advocate that, truly, truly, age is a number, and it's how you feel, and how healthy you are, and how you take care of yourself, and what's your mental attitude. I remember I was meeting with this Chinese director, and he's like, "Oh, I love you," and he said to me, "I wish I could find a 20-year-old like you." I looked at him, and I said, "You could probably find 50 20-year-olds," I said, "that's why you're not making money on any of your movies, but how many my age can you see doing what I'm doing?" Then he didn't say anything, so I think women deal with a lot of that, not only … It's also an age thing, and it's this and that, and I think … strong advocate. That's a pet peeve of mine. It's like … that shouldn't be.

JL: Right. I agree. There's something to be said for Hollywood and the marketability. You know, it seems like it just keeps going up for men. I mean, look at *The Expendables*. Let's collect a bunch of action stars who … for … I'm looking for diplomatic words here … they … their careers have spanned a few years.

CR: Exactly. If you look at Liam Neeson, Jason Statham, Arnold Schwarzenegger, Sylvester Stallone, those guys are action heroes. They're all older, and they all make money. It was funny, because I was like, "Why wasn't I in *The Expendables*?" I was doing movies in the 80s and

90s. Where was the woman? Why I wasn't in there? Because I should have been in there! Again, who knows what happens, but I think things happen for a reason, and if it's meant to be … I still think they should put me in one because I was the woman doing all that during that era, you know? I do think a lot of my friends my age, like Olivier Gruner, Don Wilson, Michael Jai White, they're in fantastic shape. They're healthy, we work out, and I think that attributes to our martial art training. I always say it's a warrior spirit. We always strive to do the best we can, not saying we're always doing the best, but try to be as fit as we can, as healthy as we can, as positive as we can.

Failures, everybody has failures. How do we … We deal with it. We deal with it and move on. My friend, Dr. Bob Goldman, said a speech once that stuck in my mind. He says, "I wake up and I have obstacles for breakfast." My advice to people is you have to do what makes you happy. Some people will say, "Oh, yeah, but you travel, and it costs this and that," and it's like, "No." Just the other day, I was walking outside and it was … You know when it rains, and it's just misty and you get that smell? I was in heaven. I said, "I love this," so it's just the little things, too. You've just got to really, really find things that make you happy, and maybe people that are negative, or depressed, or whatever, haven't found that, and they need to find that joy in their life to keep them positive and going.

JL: I've said it before, and I'll say it again. I have the best job in the world. Getting to talk to martial artists, especially those whom I've known about and wanted to get to know better for a very long time, what's better than that? Thank you, ma'am, for coming on the show. Thanks for chatting with me. I look forward to seeing you again.

For all of you listening, make sure you head on over to whistlekickmartialartsradio.com. Check out all the stuff that we've got going on over there, like signing up for the newsletter, and if you've listened this far into the outro, guess what? We've got a little bit of special bonus material that came after we closed the episode. Why didn't I let you know about that in the intro? Because it's only for those of you who really, really care about the episodes, and you're going to listen deep into this stuff, so yeah.

Don't forget, you've got lots of ways you can help us out, buying something, telling people about something, Patreon. It's all out there. Anything that you can do to help us grow is greatly appreciated. Oh, and don't forget, we've got a speed development program that you should probably check out at whistlekick.com. It's going to make you faster, faster than you've ever imagined. Seriously, if you follow the protocol and there you will get crazy fast.

Stick around, but until next time, this is all I have, so train hard, smile and have a great day.

CR: I know. A monkey bit me in the ear and tried to draw blood when I was in [inaudible 58:05].

JL: Wait, seriously?

CR: Yeah! I went into this thing, they put … This monkey jumped up on my shoulder, and he bit … He was gnawing on my ear. I'm like, "Can you get this monkey off my ear? He's biting me!" I started thinking, "Was it that?" Then, people are saying, "Maybe when you were diving, you got something in your …" Then I took three COVID tests, and it said negative, because the symptoms were like, it could have been … I'm vaccinated, but it could have been something like COVID, but that's … they kept coming up negative. Even now, I still … He says two to four weeks before I'm back to normal. I'm feeling good. I'm off the antibiotics, but I feel like if I try to work out, I get tired. I guess it's because the lungs are still trying to heal and whatever. That was a rough two weeks for me.

JL: I believe it.

CR: I got a little nervous there. Now, I'm … I'll tell you. I've been traveling a lot during COVID, but now, I'm a little nervous about it because that totally was not fun.

SENIOR MASTER OF THE ARTS
JEFF SPEAKMAN

"I didn't know him for a long time, then all of a sudden we started doing a lot of seminars together. He took the Kempo system and played with it and changed it, which is what we are all supposed to do. We became good friends and is a superb gentleman."

— Bill Wallace

"Jeff Speakman is known for his martial arts, his work in films, and his dedication to preserving traditional martial arts. Jeff stands for truth and integrity in the martial arts world, which I truly admire."

— Cynthia Rothrock

"He is kenpo style different than mine, but we can get along."

— Fumio Demura

Interview was originally released on April 3, 2023.

Jeremy Lesniak: Welcome. You're tuned into an episode of whistlekick Martial Arts Radio and our guest today for episode 802, Senior Master Jeff Speakman.

My name's Jeremy Lesniak. I'm your host for the show, founder of whistlekick where all we do is in support of traditional martial arts. If you are a traditional martial artist somewhere in the world and you train and you love training, I don't care what you train, where, when, why – I don't even care how, I care *that* you train – and if you are a martial artist, we make a lot of stuff. We do a lot of things in support of you and your training. If you go to whistlekick.com you can find all of them, from the events, to the training programs, to the protective equipment, to apparel. There's lots of great stuff over there. Check it out. If you use the code podcast15, it's going to save you 15% and let us know that the show leads back to selling some stuff, which business-wise is a good thing to know.

This show gets its own website because there's a lot going on for the show by itself, whistlekickmartialartsradio.com. We've got 801 episodes beyond this one for you to check out. If you're new to the show, plenty of time to fill your commute, or cleaning the house, or whatever you do when you're checking out this show. I hope that you do because it means a lot to us and our mission to connect, educate, and entertain the traditional martial artists of the world. It really resonates for the team, for myself, and for many of you.

If that resonance makes you think, "I'd love to keep these guys going. I'd love to support them," well, you could make a purchase, but you could also leave a review, and we do have a Patreon, patreon.com/whistlekick. It starts at only $2 a month and we're going to throw great stuff your way. If you like the show, you will love the stuff we do in Patreon. It's just an extension. It's a little bit more raw, uncut. Sometimes we … No, I'm not even going to tell you. You've got to go check it out, patreon.com/whistlekick.

If you've been listening a while, watching a while, if you are part of our family, you should be checking out the family page, whistlekick.com/family. It is a page we update every week with all the things you can do to help us, but it's also a place that we post some exclusive stuff you're not going to find anywhere else.

Today's guest likely needs no introduction for you, so let me introduce a little bit from *my* vantage what's happening here. As you might imagine, when we started Martial Arts Radio, when the "we" was just me – I did the booking, I did the editing, I did the posting, I did all of it. Every single thing that happened at whistlekick for quite a while was just me. There was a list. There was a list of people I wanted to have on the show, and they were big names, and we've had many of them. This is one that was on that list from Day One.

When you think about Jeff Speakman, you probably think about his movie debut, *The Perfect Weapon,* and you probably think about the way his fight scenes happened, the authenticity, the quality. In fact, *The Perfect Weapon* was the first martial arts film that I heard people talk about and point to the fight scencs and say, "That was realistic. I liked the way that was done," as opposed to a lot of the stuff through the eighties where it was slow or it was very bluntly choreographed. Not in this film. I think it's that contrast that has made him such a celebrated figure in our world, and now finally, thanks to Andrew's persistence, we have him on the show.

Whenever I have conversations with celebrity martial artists, I hope that I rise to the occasion because of the way they're showing up. I value their time, but they generally give some great stuff. This is no exception. I think you're really going to enjoy this episode, and I'll talk to you some more on the other side in the outro.

I want to thank you for coming on. I appreciate your time.

Jeff Speakman: Of course.

Lesniak: I suspect most of the audience knows who you are, so we don't really need to do a big formal intro, but I'm going to ask you to start the way that I ask nearly everyone to start. We'll let that guide where we head next and that's what was your first experience with martial arts?

Speakman: My own, personal experience is when I began in 1978, studying Japanese Gōjū-ryū from a black belt of Lou Angel, back in the Midwest where I was attending the university there. Then after a year or so of that is when I transitioned over and started to study directly from Hanshi Angel in Joplin, Missouri. Then I went on … and as you can imagine, I'm frustrated because this is not doing what I want it to do. But tell me what does?

Lesniak: Yeah, exactly.

Speakman: In the world of today's technology. I'm just trying to get this …

Lesniak: Sure.

Speakman: … organized. With any kind of luck that will work. Back to the point. It was really my experience with Lou Angel and Japanese Gōjū-ryū that was my beginning, but I sought out martial arts because in high school I was a springboard diver in the summer and a gymnast in the winter. When I left Chicago to go to college, I always wanted to do either professional dance or martial arts. I had a roommate for a year, and then a year later, I found out he was a black belt in Japanese Gōjū-ryū. I always thought, wow, that was incredible to be a friend of a guy, you live with him, you share a home, and you don't even know he has any idea about martial arts. I admired that humility I guess, and it made me very curious. He was the one that started teaching me and then eventually got me together with Mr. Angel.

Lesniak: We can certainly in hindsight see parallels between dance and martial arts, but I wouldn't imagine that too many kids in their late teens are looking at those two things as pursuits that they might want to engage in either or …

Speakman: Right as a parallel.

Lesniak: It's not a connection I think I would expect many to draw. Obviously, martial arts is where you ended up. What was it about dance?

Speakman: Well, as I was explaining, I was a springboard diver all my life and a gymnast all through high school, and a gymnast all my life. When I left that environment, I wanted to do something movement-related, but I did not want to continue on with springboard diving or on with gymnastics because it's like I've been there, done that, you know? What would be next? I'm interested in the movement and athleticism, if you will, of those two things. That was the related context that I saw those two things in. I agree that it isn't normal, but I have lived my entire life carrying the burden of not being normal. Oddly enough, it has made all the difference.

Lesniak: Now, was it choreography within gymnastics that really resonated for you? Because I could definitely see choreography into dance, and you have some understanding of martial …

Speakman: Yes.

Lesniak: Okay.

Speakman: I think it was more general than that, but I think you're quite correct. As I would describe it to you now, it would be a propensity for extreme right hemisphere behavior, so that a visual, analytical, spatial, movement-related, tied to athleticism, not just walking your dog around the block, but competitive, high-level athleticism.

I had a very difficult family life growing up, so I became very good friends with another family there, the Cashmore family. This was in Chicago, or the suburb of Chicago. Maybe you know somebody like this, but this family has such a genetic propensity to be outstanding athletes in anything that they ever did. Any one of the kids, you name it – tennis, football, gymnastics, swimming, anything – they were just amazing. I literally hung out with them every day, and we were very good friends, and we played ping pong every night in their basement.

My point of telling you that story is that was my norm. To hang around unbelievably exceptional martial artists, well, that was just like falling off a log, you know, where everybody would look at what they did, and their jaw would hit the ground. Well, that was just what they did every day, so that became my norm, that level of commitment, that idea of athleticism on that level. In other words, I was heavily predisposed. That was essentially the only thing that brought me happiness in my life all through my adolescent years, until at the age of 17, I left to go to the university, then college, now University in Joplin, Missouri. Because I was so incredibly steeped in such an extreme level of that, that was my norm. Not that I was anywhere near as good as they were, but I was just with them, and you know what? You want to get good at tennis, play with somebody that kicks your ass every day.

Lesniak: Right.

Speakman: Learn from the best, play with the best. If you want to advance yourself intellectually, hang around smart people and have the courage to shut up and sit and listen, and take in the brilliance of whom and what they are. Appreciate it, and then give yourself permission to be changed by that.

Lesniak: Well said. Because it seems like such a significant … I don't believe in coincidences, but occurrence, your attending college where you did, and ending up, as you said, living with whom you did, what was it that brought you to Joplin? I don't imagine there are a whole lot of guys graduating school in Chicago and saying, "You know, I've got to go down here."

Speakman: Yeah. There would have to be a story to that, and there is of course. My best friend at that time in high school, again, back in the suburb of Chicago, his family bought a small ranch in a very small town,

45 minutes south of the small city of Joplin, Missouri, so he was attending that college. I stayed in contact with him.

I was at the end of graduating from high school and hated my life and hated being home, and I had to get out of there. I had to get out. He said, "Look, why don't you move down here? I have an extra bedroom in my house. You can live here. If you use this as your residency and then get accepted at that college and … just live here and figure it out from there." I went, "Okay sounds good." I then sold my car to pay for the U-Haul and I moved down there, and that's where it took me.

For my first semester, I fed a couple of dozen head of cattle every single morning, 5:30 in the morning, rain or shine or snow. I was out there feeding cattle that paid for my room and board on their ranch.

Lesniak: Okay. I've had the experience of teaching and, just as I'm sure you have and many others, teaching folks who have a lot of time in with some kind of physical pursuit – diving, gymnastics. Sometimes those folks really take to martial arts training because they're willing … they can let go. Other times it's really difficult to get them to move their body in this new way because they're so comfortable moving in this other way. Which were you?

Speakman: I was already moving that way. When I fell in love with martial arts right away, and then had the opportunity to learn directly from and become a black belt under Lou Angel, I ate that with a spoon. I immediately felt like … Well, here's the conclusion I drew at that time. I said, "I'm going to do this all my life." Of course, I had no idea how or where I was going to wind up here, but right from the time I began, I was very, very committed to the martial arts.

I was just so incredibly fortunate to be in this really, very small city in the middle of the Midwest – this was 1976, by the way – and to have found a guy like Lou Angel. What are the chances of that? What else is interesting is he was retired from teaching. He was the night sergeant at a police department outside of Joplin, Missouri, which was well known for being an extremely rowdy troublesome little community. He was the troubleshooter. When there was trouble, they sent Angel out to take care of it.

My first lessons with Lou Angel … This little township was called Webb City. My first experience with Lou Angel was down in the abandoned jail cell basement of the Webb City, Missouri Police Department, abandoned for a long time, one light bulb hanging down from the string in the ceiling, cement walls, old iron doors. We worked out in a cell, and he had a dummy in the corner and a couple of guys that were his black belts or whoever that came over and trained with him occasionally, and that's where he started teaching me. Then probably about a year after that, he got reinvigorated and went back and reopened his school called The Academy of Self-Defense.

Lesniak: Wow. I mean that sounds like it's straight out of a movie.

Speakman: It's nuts. Yeah. I mean, if you put that in a movie, people are going to go, "Oh, brother. Really?" You know? But it really was true.

Lesniak: Yeah. But that would never happen.

Speakman: Yeah, exactly. Let me follow that just a little bit further.

Lesniak: Yeah.

Speakman: Just to give you an idea of how I was raised in the martial arts, when you're in a traditional martial art as opposed to a nontraditional – I was in both – when I was in a traditional, Japanese Gōjū-ryū was being done exactly the way it was done 400-plus years ago, and you wouldn't deviate from it. You're never welcome to raise your hand and say, "Excuse me? What does that mean? Or how would you do that here? Or that?" You would be … You would drop and do 40 pushups. If you were in a tournament and you were doing a point tournament, and you were sure you scored the point, and the other guy got the point, if you even went, "Uh …" like that, you were immediately kicked out, taken out. If you actually went a little bit further than that, you were thrown out of the association. The patch was ripped off your gi and you were out for the rest of your life.

I actually failed twice going up the ranks, including my last one, which was for nidan ho, which is the second half of the second-degree black belt in the Japanese systems. You've got first, second, and third degree actually have a first part of it and the second part of it. The shodan ho, shodan, nidan ho, nidan, on and on. It only has fourth degree black belt. You go to one belt moving forward. Anyway, the reason I failed, the second time was we have a kind of tension-breathing kata, where you come out like this [demonstrates] and you exhale, and it's a very strong, slow-motion, body tension. It's called Sanchin is the name of the kata. Then there's a bit of Sanchin-kind of movement in the brown belt kata called Kensho. I did all that and then I finished that kata, and Mr. Angel stood up and he said, "Okay bow to me, and go sit down." That's the only way you knew how you failed. You want to know what you did wrong? You've got to show up and come to class the next day, which of course I did, and the reason I failed is because in my exhale of that moment in Kensho where you're doing a slow-motion tension thing, my breathing was too loud, and so he failed me for that reason.

Lesniak: Wow.

Speakman: Now that's the norm that I grew up in.

Lesniak: Yeah.

Speakman: Then I come to California to study Kenpo, and I'm immediately immersed in that world. I'm trying to scramble to learn what's this about? How do you guys do this and that? I'd get overwhelmed by, I don't know, 40, 50 times the information necessary to go to black belt in Kenpo than in Gōjū-ryū. The differences are indescribable and they're very difficult because the stances are different, the thinking is different. You name it, it's different, so was a monstrous challenge.

Then I eventually became a student directly under Ed Parker. Now, I wound up going to Kenpo because Lou Angel knew Parker from back in the day, and he wrote me a letter of introduction. In '83, I moved to California once again, sold my car to pay for the U-Haul, lived with a friend there, and found Mr. Parker at the International Championship in Long Beach, which was the granddaddy of all tournaments back in the day. Walked up to him, bowed, and handed him this letter. He opened the letter and said …

Lesniak: At the tournament?

Speakman: At the tournament. Yep. I walk into this tournament in the Long Beach arena, this gargantuan … thousands of people in stadium seating with rings all over. You can imagine what that looked like to a guy that just came from Joplin, Missouri. I was like, "What is this?"

I kept asking people, "Where is Ed Parker? Where can I find him?" Eventually, I found him, bowed very deeply to show my respect, gave him the letter. He read it and said, "Oh, you're from my old friend Lou Angel. Here's my home phone number. Call me in a couple of weeks when I'm done with all this and I'll get you set up," and that's how I started.

Lesniak: Being that … I'm imagining you're coming from these disciplines that have a fair amount of rigidity and consistency and you end up in …

Speakman: Extremely.

Lesniak: … Gōjū-ryū, which anybody who's trained Gōjū-ryū knows that's a good way of describing that, and you come into Kenpo at a time where … I wasn't there then, but my understanding historically is that it was a time of rapid evolution for Kenpo. Was that difficult for you to step into when I would imagine, across a six-month span, things are changing?

Speakman: Yeah. It was ex-

Lesniak: "This isn't like this anymore. It's like this now."

Speakman: Yeah. Right. It was extremely challenging. Even if that continuing evolution and change that you are correctly referring to wasn't there, it would still be like sticking your finger in a light socket and going, "What the …?!" You know. It was so incredible. We would do … From the perspective I had at that time, we would do things, techniques, and they were so brutal and so what I would have then called overkill – I now call over-skill – but it was just astonishing. You couldn't have things more in a bipolar atmosphere.

Then about '85, '86 is when I was asked by Ed Parker to go to his house every week with three other people and become a private student, which I never thought that would ever happen. I just happened to be in Texas when he was there. I went to his seminar, of course, and that's when he told me to not go to the West LA school – which was managed by Larry Tatum at that time – anymore, start coming to his house. It wasn't like, "Come to my house *and* go there." "Don't go there anymore. Just come to my house," which was a bizarre thing, of course. I didn't ask why, because you don't ask why.

Lesniak: Do you know why now?

Speakman: Oh, I learned why shortly thereafter, and I know why now as well, but I did exactly what he said.

Lesniak: Of course.

Speakman: But the point I think I want to make sure I make clear is when I first showed up in Kenpo, it was version 1.0, and it was literally called that. There were 32 techniques per belt, and it was an insane amount. It's still an insane amount of material, but it was even more insane then.

Then, when I went in Mr. Parker's house in '85 or '86 … '85, I think, that all changed and it shifted to version 2, which was 24 techniques. It was spread out much longer, so then not only were the number of

techniques not … You didn't change … They would just spread it out.
It was the same techniques spread out, but he actually altered many of
the techniques, changed a lot of the extensions, finished different forms.
This was version 2.0, which was the more updated version of Kenpo,
and that is what I learned from him. I saw and I personally experienced
Kenpo 1.0 and then Kenpo 2.0, so I could see that arc. Because I got to
know him so well, I understood how he thought to create that evolution
and that change.

Now, fast forward to today, actually back in 2005, that's how it was … I
and all my group with me were able to take the Kenpo 2.0 and change it
to 3.0, 4.0, and eventually in 2005, came to this thing we do now called
Kenpo 5.0, because I knew how he thought. I was in the presence of a
brilliant man. I could see it from a mile and a half away, and I just shut
up, as I mentioned earlier, and I just tried to absorb this unbelievable
amount of information coming from the mouth and the mind of a guy
whom I referred to as the Einstein of Martial Arts. He was so brilliant in
what he did. If I may …

Lesniak: Please.

Speakman: … what I mean by that is, when you read about Einstein or
the other incredible brains of humanity, the one thing that you see that
they all have in common is they're able to look at exactly the same
situation, if you will, and see something completely different. Many
other brilliant people are looking at the same thing and they don't get it.
Some people can do that. If you find somebody who's like that, you
should pay attention, you should follow that person, because that's
somebody with a big enough brain to be a leader that you want to
emulate, follow that cognitive pathway, and in this case also a physical
pathway.

Because I recognize that, I just absorbed every little bit that I could over
those years, going to his house every week. Then I got the job. I was
studying acting for five years. I got the job in *The Perfect Weapon* with
Paramount, which I then brought him in with me and we shared that
experience together. We spent many, many hours talking about what he

would like to see because I had control of the fight scenes, and I had the final edit and soundcheck of the fight scenes. As amazing as that is, throw this on top of it, that was my first movie.

Lesniak: Right.

Speakman: Who's going to give a first-time guy that kind of authority and control? That was actually given to me by Paramount after the movie was done because they wanted to add some scenes and they had a miserable experience with the guy that was the director-producer of that, Mark DiSalle, who produced Van Damme's first three movies, which is how he was able to take me and go into Paramount. They didn't want to use him in that, so they came to me.

Then, when I was watching the edited scenes of the movie, I was saying, "You know, this is missing and this doesn't belong there, that should be here not there," and I'm saying that, and they go, "Ok, how about if you give it a shot?" I've never set foot in an editing bay. I said, "Great. I would love to." I went in, did that, changed all the fight scenes. Sitting with very, very accomplished intelligent people, I would go, "I know we have that on the other side," you know, when they turn the cameras around and shoot from the B side, "and that's what should go right there," and he went, "Oh, that's where that belongs." You've got to admit, there's so much stuff going on in the middle of a Kenpo fight scene, certainly in *The Perfect Weapon*, it would be very easy for you to go, "Okay, I didn't know the technique was supposed to be that. Now I know." I brought a lot of linear feet of the fight scene that were thrown in the trashcan, I brought it back out …

Lesniak: Right.

Speakman: … and put it in, which expanded the fight scene. Those are the things that cost the most, so the more seconds you can get on camera on the final product of the fight scenes, the more money value you're getting.

Lesniak: Right.

Speakman: They just got thrown in the trash can, and now you're pulling them out of the trash can, and therefore you're giving better bang for the buck, if you will, to the producers, and in this case, the studio.

Lesniak: And this explains why for so many people, *The Perfect Weapon* was the first truly quality martial arts film in terms of the fight choreography and in terms of what we saw on screen. Obviously, you cared about it because you invested that time. I'm curious, how much of that caring was you as a martial artist, and how much was you as the star wanting to deliver a great result?

Speakman: Well, it was first then and is now, and will be as long as I'm on planet Earth, martial arts first. I was a martial artist first, then the movie star thing came and went. Maybe I'll go back one day again, maybe not. I don't know, but the through line since 1978 – back when the Earth was cooling – is that I'm a martial artist, first, second, and third, but your point is, yes, I also cared as the lead of the film, and I cared what it'll look like because the respons- … and this is really huge. Imagine this on your shoulders. The responsibility of making sure that the fight scenes are accurate and done well and represent the art well. I mean, this is the first "Kenpo movie."

Lesniak: Right.

Speakman: Now the responsibility on my shoulders of representing that correctly, and most importantly, the way Mr. Parker wanted it, was enormous. I had to go in and prove that I could add value and therefore a better return on investment. If you let me do what I do, I'm going to get the best bang from the book. That stayed through the rest of the nine movies I starred in. I always had contractually the right to choreograph and have final edit and final sound check on all of the fight scenes. If they didn't want to do that, I didn't do the movie.

There was a time where Warner Brothers had me on a holding deal for a year to do a TV series, so we signed that deal, everything was great. We start getting into the development of it, and when we approach the subject, it's, "Ok, but I need to have control of the fight scenes," even though it's a weekly television show at that time. They said, "Well, we don't give that authority to actors." This was Warner Brothers. I said, "Okay, great. Here's a crazy idea. Give me another title. Don't pay me any more. Just give me whatever title you need to give me so that I can have the approval." Remember, all I'm asking for is the ability to add value to the film, or in this case the TV show, and in that equation was, and I can't interfere with the delivery schedule. I said, "Okay, I can help train a guy or two guys or a team of people to edit the fight scenes correctly, and then you can have at it all you want, because they're still accurately representing what the art is," but they wouldn't even do that.

Lesniak: Why?

Speakman: I said, "Well, okay, if you change your mind, call me." It really goes to corporate culture. When Warner Brothers came to me, they said, "We don't do that." I was not sarcastic, although I am in many things most of my life, I wasn't then. I said, "Okay, great, I understand that. What I'm trying to say is, BUT if we're going to work together, I've got to have that, so you tell me what you need to be able to give me that because that's not a negotiable point." They were, "Who the heck are you? We're Warner Brothers." I said, "Okay, then you can keep it," which what actor given, you know, would turn that down, but I never sold out.

I never sold out. Even now in my association, and we're in 21 countries, we're the largest Kenpo organization internationally in history, I still won't give. You can talk to my student in Holland and Bolivia and Australia and New Zealand. They'll tell you, if you're going to walk this walk and you're going to wear this belt, you're going to earn it just like I did.

The good news is I've tested for all of my belts, including this 10th-degree black belt I'm wearing. I never got a promotion. I got out with my students in line and tested. That's the good news. The bad news for them is now it's your turn. If I did it, you're going to do it. Now, that's going to attract a certain kind of person, and that's going to repel many other people. My point is, I don't care. You can stay or you can go. I'm not vying for students. I'm looking for a kind of person. It doesn't matter what language you speak, what color your skin, what religion you belong to, what your sexual preferences or your sexual orientation. All those walls of illusion that everybody sets up and lives their entire life by, none of those exist in our association. The only judgment that exists is the content of your character, and I judge that by how you treat the other people in our organization and how you treat your students. I am much, much more impressed with that than I am with the physical stuff.

Now, what's really, really unique and great about what we've accomplished in Kenpo 5.0 is we have both. We have amazing, wonderful human beings that want to make the world a better place, who happen to be first-rate martial artists, Kenpoists, and human beings at the same. I never thought, honestly, I never thought we would be as big as we are right now because who would want to … That's a lot of work.

Lesniak: Yeah.

Speakman: You would have to sacrifice a lot. Before I had all the videos and everything done, I still had people in Australia and Bolivia and all throughout Europe. I would see them once or twice a year and they would still rise to the occasion and live by the standard. Now of course we have internet, and I put all of the system on the website. We actually have an online university. Not only all the schools, but every single student around the world has access to the videos and the written version of not only the techniques but the sets and the forms. If you're sitting in Italy having lunch and you pull out your cell phone, you can see whatever it is you want to see 24/7.

Lesniak: I don't think you can overstate the contributions that Ed Parker made to the world of martial arts.

Speakman: No question.

Lesniak: You certainly have acknowledged his greatness and even gone a bit further than I've heard others go in elevating him. Really, what I'm finding interesting is you acknowledge and maybe even, to a certain degree, create these very big shoes that eventually you stepped into. I'm wondering if that came with any sort of apprehension.

Speakman: I'm not sure I would associate apprehension. I would certainly associate the word responsibility and overwhelming responsibility.

Lesniak: Sure.

Speakman: Then the bombastic audacity to actually change the art to take it from 4.0 to 5.0, which was …

Lesniak: You said something there that I was not able to say, so yes, thank you for going there because that's a fairly bold thing to do, to say how brilliant this man is, let me change some of the stuff he did.

Speakman: Well, yes, except that was not only who he was and was always like that, because that's how we got from Kenpo 1.0 to 2.0 to 3.0 to 4.0 was him changing and evolving the art, but if you read anywhere of any of his works … Let me give you a quote, which is one of the quotes we lean on to justify what we've done, which is … Again, this is an Ed Parker quote. "The ignorant refuse to study and the intelligent never stop. A real martial artist pursues change. He doesn't fear it." It was his mandate that his black belts continue to change and evolve the art to keep it relative.

Even another quote from his was, "When I'm gone, I hope no one traditionalizes my art," and much to my staggering surprise and disappointment, virtually everybody did exactly what he asked you not to do. No one evolved it. No one changed it. If you had a hundred Ed Parker black belts in the room and say, "Ok, everybody, raise your hand to evolve the art," probably five hands would go up and mine would be one. Then you go, "Ok, of you five guys, who would advance the art to try to include ground fighting?" Four hands drop, and mine stays up because my read of where we were, to keep Kenpo relevant so it doesn't become obsolete, is to approach the 800-pound gorilla in the room, which the Gracie Brothers – and I'm very grateful to them – and eventually the Machado family brought to this country that version of Brazilian jiujitsu, which morphed into this acronym we have now called MMA.

Imagine all through the sixties and seventies and even into the eighties, Kenpo was clearly recognized as the street martial art until the Gracies showed up, and then we got it shoved down our throat like everybody else. You would be very hard-pressed to find somebody more grateful to them and the Machado family than I am because they enlightened us the hard way, but they enlightened us on what we didn't know.

Then the wake-up call was, "Okay guys, Mr. Parker's gone, but if you want to do something about Kenpo maintaining its position as the street fighting martial art, we'd better … because if we don't approach this, we're going to get creamed," and we got creamed. Then I said, "Okay, you're not going to do it, so I'm going to do it." Well, when I did it, then I received a huge amount of pushback from not only much of the Kenpo community but from many of the seniors who I knew.

Now, fast forward to these more current days, let's say the last 10 years, my position with those same people is, what are you doing? You have looked at 18 years of what I've done and successfully created, and it's a solution. Whatever it is you want to see, we've done it, and yet you do nothing, including, then, that means, in participating in doing exactly what Ed Parker asked you not to do.

Lesniak: Right. Well, why do you think that is?

Speakman: Big, big question, with different answers that almost compete with one another. One of them, which is actually in defense of those people who refuse to change, and that is that you just have to remember in the seventies and the eighties and even going into the nineties, communication was absolutely nothing like what it is not just today, but in the last 10 years.

Lesniak: Yeah.

Speakman: The dissemination of the material and the information was one-twentieth of what it is today or less, just because the communication standard wasn't there. Back then, the web wasn't built. Nobody had a pc, there were no cell phones. Now we have many computers that are cell phones. The rate of change through that technology has been greater in the last five years than the last 50, and greater in the last 10 than the last 100. In a way, to defend what I now call apathy is that it just wasn't there. Those standards, that information, that communication, it wasn't available to you even if you wanted it, even if you sought it out. If you wanted to, you had to get on a plane and go to California, and many people did do that, much to all of their credit.

Now when you move forward into today's world where we can communicate on that level, we can learn, we can evolve, and they choose not to, in my opinion, is doing a tremendous disservice to Ed Parker, to the art of Kenpo and to the potential of who we could be as an organized group.

Lesniak: Of those, you know, you gave the metaphor a hundred people in a room, five of them are trying to move Kenpo forward, the other 95 are not raising their hand. Over the course of the work that you've been doing, how many of those 95 have taken it as a kick in the butt and started doing anything? Has it inspired anybody?

Speakman: None that I'm …

Lesniak: Really?

Speakman: None that I'm aware of. That came from the generation I came from. There's that language out there, first-generation Parker, which of course there were lists and lists of all the people that were black belts from Ed Parker long before I ever walked in the door, but the nomenclature definition of that category is, if you're a personal black belt under Ed Parker from whatever year, you're a first-generation Parker black belt. Okay, that would fit me, but I don't want that. I want to be known as the last generation, not the first generation, which would be important only in Kenpo. If it was Gōjū-ryū, it would be the opposite, it would be a negative, but in an art that's evolving, changing, growing, and the mandate and the edict is advance, change, and grow, "Even after I'm gone, guys," then the idea that you're changing and growing is the point.

On one hand, it's easy to understand how the older guys don't. On the other hand, it's very difficult for me to comprehend why they don't because you knew Ed Parker, in some cases 20 years longer than I did, and you say openly that you were his student and you were close to him, and this is how we all wanted it done, blah blah. Okay, great, but then why haven't you changed? Why haven't you adapted the solution base of how to do your Kenpo on your back, which is what Kenpo 5.0 is?

There could have been many, and there are other people who are doing that, but they're just not First-Generation Parker. The question begs, why not? What is it that you missed? I could phrase it in the way that I phrase it, which is, how could you be around a great man like that, which I refer to as the Einstein of Martial Arts, and not get who he was? They go, "What do you mean?" Well, because if you got who he was, you would've changed and evolved the art. You're showing me by your apathy that you're not interested in evolving and changing the art. You just want to keep it going.

Once again, in an attempt to try to defend them, I would say, I get it and I understand it because since you haven't evolved and changed and addressed grappling and how to figure out how to do it in Kenpo and meld those two worlds together, your population is declining rapidly, because … Pick a 17-year-old kid who walks in and sees a Kenpo school and goes, "Wow, that's really amazing. Well, what about on the ground? How do you get out of this or that, or that?" They go, "Oh, well, we don't do ground fighting here." "Great, thank you. Goodbye."

Unless you address that situation in a very meaningful way, you're going to do "this" and we are doing "that." Once again, I can kind of understand why you don't like me, and to be honest with you, if it wasn't me, I probably wouldn't like me either, but that's not the case.

Lesniak: Right.

Speakman: Because I went through my stage four cancer in 2013, it took two years for me to get my mojo back, which is a flip of a coin if you're going to live or not, but one of the things that happened when I came out, I said "Okay, I'm not drinking the Kool-Aid any more. We're not doing this. I am no longer going to step back and go, 'Well, maybe they won't like it if I …'" I went, "Okay, like it or love it or hate it, either way, I'm going ahead." That is when we really took off on a worldwide …

What was surprising to me was I thought maybe I would lose 10, 15, 20% of my student base. Well, the opposite happened. It was like they were like, "It's about time. We've been waiting for you to get over yourself so we can move on." Once that had happened, the illumination of the way forward was very clear to me, so I moved forward with that because I came out of really close to being dead. You look at it and you go, "Okay, what am I going to do with whatever heartbeats are left?"

I'm 65 now. It's been 10 years since my cancer, and if everything remains really good, I'm going to be dead in somewhere between 20 and 30 years, so let's work from that paradigm back and go, "Okay, I've got 20 to 30 years of being alive, maybe 20 years of being physically active, maybe 10. I don't know. What am I going to do? What are you going to do? How are we going to help move things forward?

My message to the rest of the Kenpo community world is give yourself permission to step out and to be great and to be a part of something great. Maybe you like what we do, maybe you don't. Either way, I'm good with that, but if you want to operate on the very, very high level, do the entire art.

Once again, in an attempt to show my ignorance, I went for 39 years after the death of Ed Parker assuming – of course, really because of where I came from, which I've explained to you, with Lou Angel – that every single person who was a fourth-degree black belt or higher would know our Form Seven, the stick form, or fifth-degree black belt and higher would know the Form Eight, which is the Knife Form. For 39 years, I just assumed you and everybody else did.

I start looking around going, "Why is it for the last 25 years, no one asks me to come and sit on their testing board or to give seminars at their school or whatever?" I always thought it was because they didn't like what I did by evolving the art and the arrogance of it all and blah blah, blah. That may very well be true, but now 39 years later, I'm highly suspect that it's because they don't do the basic minimum requirements for fourth- and fifth- and higher degree black belt.

If I'm sitting on your testing board and you're going for fifth, I'm going to raise my hand and say, "Excuse me, could I see Form Eight?" Then there's going to be some kind of answer like, "Well, we don't do Form Eight." Then I'm going to go like this and look down over at their instructor and go, "Why don't you do Form Eight?" The answer to that question is, "Well, we don't like, it because there's a problem with this and that, and that and that," and I would agree. We actually created a new Form Eight, but then the next question, which is why I've really become the Kenpo heretic is because I turn and I say, "Well, what have you done to fix it?"

Lesniak: Right.

Speakman: Yeah, and no one answers that question. Then sometimes they go, "Well, the guy who, or girl who, taught me, our association, we just don't do it." "Okay, what have the people or the heads of your organizations done to fix that problem and evolve Kenpo?" "Nothing." Well, where is the leadership in that? Based only on the edict that was sent forth from Ed Parker to evolve and change the art so it doesn't become obsolete.

There is no pretty answer to that, so instead of inviting an ugly discussion, you just marginalize me and just keep me from interacting with your students. Doing shows like this changes that dynamic greatly because there's only so much in today's world with the technology where we are experiencing right at this moment that you can marginalize somebody. If the logic and the ownership and the understanding of who Ed Parker was and the evolution we have done, if you see that as what Kenpo really truly is, then the argument that we can have is, "I just don't like what you did," or, "I don't like how you lead," or, "I don't like how you think." Okay, great. Tell me, because you'll help me be a better instructor, a better teacher, a better person. Give it to me, lead me. I'm looking for …

Lesniak: It's far more conducive.

Speakman: … leadership all the time, and I don't see it.

Lesniak: Given that you've spent so much time thinking about this and immersed in this kind of root problem of the vast minority of Ed Parker students not taking his edict and moving it forward, not evolving and changing the art, I can only imagine that you've put some time into thinking, how do you make sure that your students do continue to change and evolve the art. You brought up your timeline, so I'm going to guess that a simple edict is not strong enough and you've probably built something stronger into what you're doing, and I'm curious what that is.

Speakman: Very much so. Thank you for asking that, because that's super important, inculcated throughout our entire system, thinking application, is the contributions that I demand from my students back to the system. You can go to any one of my schools, any one of my black belts anywhere in the world, and visit with them like we're visiting now, and they will all within reason tell you that they feel a part of the association, of the energy that we've created, of the lifestyle in this, for lack of a better expression, this utopian society that we live in called the 5.0 Family. They are co-contributors to that on a very, very big scale, and here's the deal. They know that. They feel that internally.

That is how I built this international association, through the principles of behavioral management, which was my undergraduate degree back, way back, but I'm now currently attending Purdue University Graduate School for Behavioral Sciences. I'm moving forward with my education, so that it would help me move forward with my next career move, which is motivational speaking on this topic, on this subject, for big international companies who want to increase the productivity of their employees, the problem-solving, how to create a positive feedback loop in your environment, which also helps the retention of your employee base, which is also a cost-saving thing because fewer people leave your organization because when they do, then you have to train somebody and that's a very costly thing. If we can create an environment based on positive reinforcement that makes you want to stay, it's better for your corporation. That's where I'm moving now.

I sat down to write a book called *Leadership in the Martial Arts: A Scientific Behavioral Approach.* Then I stopped and I thought, "You know what? I should go back to school and advance my education and bring it up and give me greater credulity to move forward in my new chosen field." I've already had one experience, last October of 2022 for the Emerson Electric Company, which is a Fortune 200 Company. I spoke in this way, and used the video which I've sent on to you for my opening, and they really loved it. It was huge.

Then, I've now been approved as a motivational speaker for the Morgan Stanley Investment Corp, and I'm just waiting for my first date. I live in Las Vegas, which is where I am now. They said it'll probably be in LA, but if this works, then we're on Internationally, and that's what I want. I spend every November in Europe because we have our 5.0 fighter competition. We have our own system of fighting, so we have a European, and Australasia for Australia, New Zealand, South America, and Bolivia, and then the World Championship every July here in Las Vegas, along with three regional tournaments in the US. When we have that, I go to Europe for a month, and so while I'm there I could be teaching seminars and giving … motivational speaking to different international corporations. That is my goal and my dream and my desire, and I'm taking the action to move forward in that direction.

Lesniak: Whoa. Whenever I talk to a guest who has taken their martial arts out into some other avenue of the world, inevitably, if we dig enough, we find that there are things through their nonmartial pursuits that come back into their martial arts. I would imagine that through your education, through this speaking gig, the future speaking gigs, there are things that you're already identifying that you're going to pull back in, whether it's to curriculum or to the way you teach or to your organization. I'm wondering if you might speak on those.

Speakman: Yes. At the risk of being redundant, the organization was really built on the logical, daily, practical application of basic behavioral management modification that I'm very familiar with, and because of the success rate I had in understanding those principles and putting 'them into action, that's what has coalesced our group. That's the message I can take out and help other companies build a similar thing, so there's the bridge, back from education over to martial arts, back from martial arts back over to education, and crossing back and forth.

We have, all the time in my association, different meetings, Zoom classes. When they come into Las Vegas every year in July for our big event, we have a school owners' meeting after, so I'm always talking, teaching, not only about the logic and the science and the physics and the application of Kenpo, but the logic and the science and the physics of the application of the behavioral sciences, which helps you run your school.

All of our schools are very successful. We have many schools with over 200 students in them now all around the world. The two biggest schools in Bolivia belong to us. It's helping those students to understand how to employ the basic principles and physics of behavioral management. In turn, it has made their businesses more successful, created a positive environment in their business, and generated back to the people they interact with.

We all equally understand that our interplay and interaction in this 5.0 family is actually creating literally a utopian society that we can believe in, that we can live in and work in and finish out our lives in, in a world we created. We co-created this world. It isn't me at the top of the mountain forcing everybody to bow to my feet when I walk in. I'm just not that kind of person. I actually despise that kind of mentality. On the other hand, we have to have structure and discipline and standards, and those are crystal clear, absolutely clear. Now we put them all on video and send them around the world. It's full transparency. It's a complete evolution, tackling the 800-pound gorilla in the room, which is how to do your Kenpo on your back, and adapting and changing the system to bring that reality in.

If you were to stop into one of our school, mine, for example, in Las Vegas, and you would sit and watch class while we're doing our ground stuff, it would look just like an MMA class, passing the guard, and escaping from a rear naked choke, and all the things that are associated with it, but it really isn't MMA Monday, Tuesday, and Kenpo Wednesday, Thursday. It isn't that. It's an integration of the kind of ground fighting that we would do in Kenpo that's different than what jujitsu or MMA does for one simple reason. Those things are a sport. We are not.

I learned what your rules were and then we created techniques that violate your rules, so that at the end of it all, if there was a happy outcome for the Kenpo 5.0 student against an MMA guy in the street and that guy came back a week or two weeks later and said, "What the heck was that? You kicked me in the groin, and you poked me in the trachea, and that's the only reason I lost the fight?" You would say, "Actually, that is the reason you lost the fight, because that's what we do, because we're a martial art. You don't do it because you're a martial sport."

I'm not telling you one's any better than the other. If one of us stepped in the fighting sport arena … me, for example, I would get killed. If I stepped into a jujitsu tournament. I would get wiped out. If I went into a boxing ring with a boxer, I would get creamed in no time. I don't want to live in your world. I have created a world I want to live in, and that world is based on how to fight people like you outside of your world.

Now, many of my students do participate in MMA and Jujitsu tournaments, and they step out of the Kenpo 5.0 into that world and then step back out of that and into our world. The only thing I say is, "I don't want you to become that world because in that world you must cause a person to fall for you to gain." That's competition. That's in every competition, including ours, 5.0 Fighter, but that's not what this is about. A martial fighter lives like that. A martial artist would actually sacrifice something of himself to help someone else advance. You see, that's completely antithetical, so what I say is, we live in that world, but we might have to go into that world. I don't want to fight, but I might have to, and if I do, I'm going to bring everything I've got because, as Mr. Parker said, in the street, it doesn't matter who's right, but who's left, whoever's standing. If you train like that, and I can read the signals of some guy that maybe he's a jujitsu MMA fighter, the first thing in my mind is he doesn't check or protect his groin. In Kenpo from day one, the first technique you learn is how to kick somebody in the groin, and then it gets worse after that.

We do have a window of opportunity where it could be highly effective. But in addition to that, I needed to bring the skillset of, "Oh, and by the way, if that doesn't work, then what the heck do I do while I'm pulled into somebody else's guard?" We needed to answer that, which meant we had to change the art.

Lesniak: Where else have you pulled material from? I would imagine it's from other martial arts as well. I imagine that, maybe not your goju experience, but that there are elements from other traditional arts that you've looked at and said, "I want to pull this, I want to pull this ..."

Speakman: Most ... and you're quite correct, but probably none of them came from traditional martial arts.

Lesniak: Okay.

Speakman: We have borrowed heavily from Jujitsu, from MMA, from all that world. I even was a Jujitsu student for four years in LA under a gentleman by the name of Todd Nathans, and I was so very, very fortunate to find him because he's amazing at what he does, but more importantly, he's a good person, a really good person, and all he wants to do is help people. When I walked in, as I'm sure you've heard many stories about people who start Jujitsu, they all get hurt. They get their wrist broken, they get their knee jacked up, whatever. There was none of that mentality in his school. They didn't have to. They were so talented they didn't have to shove it down your throat.

Now I did get hurt, of course, but a little bit. No one tried to hurt me, but I learned by … I wore a white gi and a white belt, and I was the other white meat. I just went in there and threw it down and was just so fortunate that I found this particular man and his dojo in LA.

Now, there were also many of my other students who all their lives were wrestlers, got into Jiujitsu and into MMA, and then there were several really good Kenpo guys in years passed who left Kenpo because of this void, this vulnerability of being taken to the ground and not knowing what to do. They left and they went into Jujitsu and MMA. When they found out what we were doing, they looked at it and then they came back. This is all over the world.

Now, when they came back, they brought their skill level and knowledge of how to fight on the ground and et cetera, et cetera, so we were, I was able, we were all able to bring all of that information, and then we evolved Kenpo 5.0 again. In 2005 is when we started 5.0. In about 2014 is when we began the process of evolving 5.0 again, so technically we actually teach 5.0.2, so it means maybe there could be a 5.0.3. I don't know. As things evolve and change, we will match that.

Lesniak: I come from a world of technology, computer science, programming, and so these version numbers, I had wondered until you made that comment just now how much you thought about them and, to folks in the audience who may not know, the closer to the dot, the more significant the evolution. A 5.0 to a 6.0 is a big deal. A 5.0 to a 5.1 is less significant. A 5.0 to 5.0.1 is even less significant.

Speakman: Right.

Lesniak: Do you think there will be a 6.0?

Speakman: There won't be in my lifetime under my tutelage, but I'm encouraging my students. I encourage everybody. If you want to take it to 5.0.3, 5.0.4, if you want to take it to 6.0 or 8.0, go for it. If other people look at what I've done, and they go, "I can do better than that," show me. Go do it. Where are you? What have you been doing for the last 10 years, 20 years? What contributions have you made to the evolution of an art whose mandate is to evolve and change over time?

Now, I totally and completely respect people who don't want to change. I came from a traditional art, so I know that mentality very well, but as time goes on and you refuse to change and try to find a way to make your Kenpo work against people who are well trained, even moderately trained on the ground, if you don't and you or one of your students are taken to the ground in a street fight by one of those guys, it'll be a humiliating experience, because the first thing I learned about Jiujitsu is take the very best Kenpo guy you can think of with the ferocity and the violence to do our striking art of Kenpo standing up as good as anybody or better, take that level and throw it on the ground and that's what Jujitsu is.

You think because somebody goes to take you down, you're going to just poke him in the eye or bite him, or, "I won't let him take me down?" That's a laughable position. More importantly, it's dangerous, because if you take that and pass that mentality onto your students and they have a false sense of security and they're taken down and they're trashed, then they're going to come back to you and go, "Okay, why didn't we do this?" You will find out the hard way what Jujitsu and MMA can do. Even though they're the best in the circumstances, which we feel we are, you might have a 50-50 chance of being able to survive that under the best of circumstances, so don't kid yourself. You keep doing your Kenpo picking low-hanging fruit and you run into the wrong guy, that is not going to be pretty.

What I'm telling you is, first, I'm 65 years old and I'm past cancer, so I don't have much gas in the tank anyhow, but even though, if I'm taken down by somebody and I pull every trick in the bag that I know of the 5.0 system, even at best, that's how good they are. Now, if you're an MMA fighter, the condition that you're in, the athletic condition that you're in is the best in the world. Fatigue makes a coward of any man.

You don't want to look at the reality of the way things are. You want them to be the way things … the way you want them to be. I empathize with that. I understand it. I don't like the world the way it is. I don't like much of anything of what's going on, but if you don't embrace change to help create the future, the one thing that will be is nothing that's important to you will be in that matrix moving forward because you didn't put it in there. Take ownership in change and evolution so you can contribute the value of what you have to offer as an intellectual, as an academic, as a fighter, as a martial artist. Pick one. Participate in the evolution and change instead of standing back and saying, "This is terrible. I want the old days." You're never going to go back. Anybody who says, "Let's take our country back," as soon as they say that, leave the room. Nobody can go backward. If somebody says, "Here's values that I want to take forward," okay, now you have my attention, but, "Let's go back to go forward," it's an impossibility. It's a preposterous, intellectually insulting position. Let's not give attention to people that are doing that. Let's give attention to people who are embracing change so they can co-create the future, not try to get us to go back.

Lesniak: Well said.

Speakman: Now, you know why a lot of people don't like me.

Lesniak: This is … You and I are of a similar mindset, which is why some people don't like me, and why I'm absolutely loving our conversation and I suspect we have others out there who are listening, watching, and going, "Yeah." How would someone … maybe they have a Kenpo school that's not affiliated with your organization and they would consider that, or maybe there's somebody who's gone lone wolf and they might want to join and find schools affiliated with you. How would they do that?

Speakman: Yep. A couple of answers to that, which are really built around this 5.0 University, Online University that we built, which as I said, every student in any country has full access to all of the information. As the consequence of that, about a year ago, we created an online academy. If you just want to stick your toe in the water, go sign up on the online academy and start learning.

If you're a Kenpo student who is in a group that doesn't want to investigate because they don't like me, they don't like change, they don't whatever, go do it anyhow. You can join the online academy in a clandestine way. Then you can learn about it, and then you see if you like it.

Then you got to know who I am through knowing my black belts, and then you can decide whether you want to be a contributor to the kind of evolution and consideration of how we live our life. If you are like that, then we are your cup of tea. If you don't want to do that, if you want to stick dogmatically to the trajectory of 15, 20, 30, 50 years ago, then you don't belong here. You're not going to like me, I'm not going to like you, so let's not waste time, just don't come over in the first place, but if you want to evolve and change and think the direction that we have headed in and the leadership that we have, the communication skills that we've developed, the business models that we have that developed moving forward, then please come and look at who we are and what we are. If you find us to be a fit, know that every single person of any race, sexual orientation, religious conviction, wherever on the globe you live, we are not judging you. The door is open and you are welcome. The price of admission is integrity.

Lesniak: How do people find all this stuff? Websites, the social media, anything like that?

Speakman: Everything is on jeffspeakman.com. You can go in … and the other great thing I should mention about the online academy is all of those lessons and instructions are archived, so you can be in Dubai on a radically different time zone and still be able to get 100% of the information. We have created the first online university like this. We've created the first 5.0 University where all the information is available and accessible to every student from the day you begin. You can log on to Jeff Speakman and see all the stuff you're learning for yellow belt with me teaching it to other students, highlighting, check this, look out for that, and here's slow motion, then I let them do it full speed, so you get … and I've re-written everything down. I rewrote every word and every page of the cumulative journal twice. The information is there, the clarity is there, and it should be a very easy and straightforward decision for you to make because we are fully transparent and open to have any kind of conversation that you're comfortable with, as long as it's respectful, of course.

Then if what I'm saying to the people who are listening right now who really didn't know what this was about, look into it and investigate and know that you're welcome, and if you don't want to do it, that's okay, too. You're still welcome to come. Our camp is open every year in July. All of our seminars around the world are completely open. For some reason, the rest of the Kenpo world has never come. They don't participate, they don't watch. I mean like one person in 20 years, that's how much of a deviation that there is.

Ironically, last year in July when I tested for my 10th, one of my dear friends in Japanese Gōjū-ryū for the first time in world history brought one of the senior black belts from Okinawa, in the Okinawan Gōjū-ryū, from the world-famous Higaonna Dojo, which as you know, that's where karate began in the world, and the very well-kept lineage, you know the Japanese people are incredibly organized and structured, so one of the senior black belts for the first time in world history came and sat on our testing board and taught seminars, and I have his signature on my tenth, which was awarded to me by Benny Urquidez. I'm sure everybody knows who that is. About two months after that, I was having lunch with him and his wife Sarah, and my wife Kim, and that's where he told me that I was the first guy he ever promoted to 10th, and I will be the last. I feel …

Lesniak: That's quite the honor.

Speakman: … the weight and responsibility and honor of that. I did the best I can to live up to that. If you don't think I deserve the 10th, if you don't think … great, call Benny Urquidez. And by the way, good luck with that, because if you know him at all, that guy speaks and lives the truth, independent of the consequences.

Lesniak: Yeah. You can't argue that man's credentials.

Speakman: Nor should you.

Lesniak: This has all been great, and thank you. I really do appreciate your time. Now it's time to wind up, and the ball's back in your court.

Speakman: Okay.

Lesniak: What are your final words for the folks listening today?

Speakman: Yeah. What I want to say is if you give too much value to pursuing the praise of other people, you will be their prisoner and you'll live out your life in subservience to something that's very much an egomaniac state. If you are looking for the kinds of things that we have to offer, please come over and look closer, and you may not like it. Although it's extremely rare, there have been a few times I've had to ask people to leave the association because the way that you conduct your life is very antithetical to how we conduct our lives and the kind of world that we have built.

You'll never be able to buy a black belt from me, so don't ask, although it happens all the time. If you want to be a part of what we do, be prepared to retest for your first- and second- and third-degree black belt all the way down the line for only one reason: everybody else did. If you have a fourth-degree black belt, do not expect to walk in and get a fourth-degree diploma from me. Embarrassingly, many people do that and they use black belt diplomas as a currency. If you come and join my organization as a fourth, I'll give you a fifth.

The only thing that's more embarrassing than that is you accept it. Instead of using that as a metric of this is exactly the person I don't want to be with, you take the fifth-degree black belt and go. Then how about people who jump rank? I know people who were a fifth, and then they go to another association, and they have an eighth. Well, you've just jumped 15 years. Why? The only answers to the questions are egocentric or solipsistic. How do you think that makes all my guys feel, who do the five-year minimums in between every belt?

Oh, and by the way, if you're with me, you've got to be in the test every year in Las Vegas, whether you're testing or not. It's four years until you're eligible for your next rank. You're going to test – full test – four times and get nothing other than the privilege and the honor of being there.

I just want to awaken all martial artists, but especially the Kenpo people out there to it very well may be that the emperor is wearing no clothes and you're afraid to make a different choice. Remember that life is very, very short under the best of circumstances. It was a flip of a coin if I was going to live past my cancer or not, and that happens to … What happened to me … There's a lot of people who aren't here anymore. Understand that the main cause of death is birth. You only have a very short time here. So don't make it about the pursuit of money and possessions and clicks on social media. It has been, is now, and forever will be the content of your character that you put on full display to how you interact with other people to make the world a better place, and then you're dead.

Lesniak: I hope you enjoyed this episode. I did. Even if you didn't, I did. Senior Master Speakman, thank you for coming on the show.

Now, what I want everybody to know is that even after we wrapped the episode, we kept talking. This is someone who I liked who I knew him to be before we talked, because I hadn't met him, but now that we've had a conversation, I like him very much. I won't go so far as to say that we are friends, but I look forward to connecting with him in the future. He's doing some remarkable things that are very much aligned with the principles we have here at whistlekick. He's taking Kenpo and moving it forward. He's taking the principles that he was given by his instructor and making improvements, something that we've talked about on this show, something that I think is very important.

Mostly I appreciate his openness, his authenticity during our conversation, because that required trust and he didn't know me from Adam before we got started. So sir, thank you. I appreciate your time. I appreciate all that you gave.

Audience, we've got a bunch of stuff you can do coming out of this episode. You've got websites to go visit. You've got things to check out whether or not you're a Kenpo practitioner. There are things that you should probably at least be aware of that we talked about today, so go to his website, see what's going on, and If you do and you start working with some of this stuff, I'd love to know it. Let me know. As always, there's no kickback, there's no commission. We don't do anything like that.

If you want to go deeper, go check out the show notes at whistlekickmartialartsradio.com. If you have a martial arts school and you would like it to grow, and you've thought about having a consultant, but maybe you're concerned about them trying to change the way you do your business or do some things out of integrity or paying a fortune for the right to have someone work with you, you should reach out because, well, we've been doing this for eight years. You know what I stand for. You know the way I run a business. You know that I do everything with integrity, and you also know that my business models always involve giving away the best stuff, so that means when we step into something like a paid consulting relationship, I'm not trying to get all your money from day one. I'd rather build a long-term relationship. You can reach out to me, jeremy@whistlekick.com or check out the consulting section under the school tab at whistlekick.com.

Okay. Seminars. I'll come teach a seminar at your school too. Let me know about that. I would love to do so. Our social media is @whistlekick, and that's it for today. Thanks for listening or watching.

Thanks for being you. Thanks for supporting us, continuing to support us.

Until next time, train hard, smile, and have a great day.

GRANDMASTER JHOON RHEE

"Probably did as much for competition as Ed Parker and Robert Trias did. Father of American TKD. We were very good friends and he was a superb gentleman. He taught Bruce Lee how to kick."

— Bill Wallace

"I've always respected and admired Jhoon Rhee's contributions to the martial arts world since I was a teen. He was an innovator and a pioneer in promoting Martial Arts."

— Cynthia Rothrock

"Very friendly with people and helps others."

— Fumio Demura

Interview was originally released on April 17, 2017.

Jeremy Lesniak: Welcome to Whistlekick Martial Arts Radio, episode 180, and thanks for tuning in. Today, we hear from Grandmaster Jhoon Rhee. Yes, THAT Jhoon Rhee.

Here at Whistlekick, we make the world's best sparring gear, and on Martial Arts Radio, we bring you the best podcast on the traditional martial arts twice every week. Welcome. My name is Jeremy Lesniak, and I'm your host as well as the founder of Whistlekick Sparring Gear and Apparel. Thank you to the returning listeners, and welcome to those of you tuning in for the very first time. You can find the show notes at WhistlekickMartialArtsRadio.com, which is also the best place to sign up for the newsletter. As a thank you for joining, we're going to send you our Top 10 Tips for Martial Artists, which is an exclusive podcast episode. We have never, will never, air that in our regular podcast feed, and our newsletter's going to keep you up-to-date on what's going on behind the scenes, tell you about upcoming show guests, and even throw you some discounts on products once in a while.

Back on episode 14, we were lucky enough to speak with Bill "Superfoot" Wallace. Some of you asked for a transcript of the show, and with permission, we've gone ahead and done that. You can find versions for both Kindle and in paperback over at Amazon.

It's hard to be in the martial arts and not know who Grandmaster Jhoon Rhee is, though there are certainly some who don't. When you talk about Taekwondo's start in the USA, you're really talking about Grandmaster Rhee. A friend of Bruce Lee, he's a central figure in a book we've spoken of many times on this show, *A Killing Art*. There's something particularly special about speaking to someone who has been training as long as Grandmaster Rhee. While not in the best of health, he was willing to take some time out of his day to speak with me about martial arts, philosophy, and his beliefs on the intersection of the two. Let's welcome him.

Grandmaster Rhee, welcome to Whistlekick Martial Arts Radio.

Grandmaster Jhoon Rhee: Oh, thank you. Thank you for invitation.

Lesniak: Thank you, sir. It's an honor and absolute privilege to speak with you.

Rhee: It's mutual.

Lesniak: Thank you. We like to talk to our guests about how they got started in the martial arts before we go off on any wanderings and start telling stories because it tends to give us context for their path, and I know that your start in the martial arts has been well-documented, and I'm sure many, many of our listeners know it, but for those that maybe haven't heard that part of your life …

Rhee: Yeah.

Lesniak: … could you tell us a little bit about how you got started with your training?

Rhee: Well, when I was 14, I had a little street fight, and I won, but I was scared, so I want to be prepared myself to not to be scared, so I entered a Chung Do Kwan right behind my home. So, another thing that is that when I finished that one week is over, I knew what I'm going to do. I'm going to go US, promote Taekwondo in the US. When I was 14, I had that decision.

Lesniak: What … Wow. Okay. I was 14 once. I've known a number of 14-year-olds, and I don't think any of them had that clear of a life plan. Why did you feel so strongly about that?

Rhee: Well, I was always longing for US, and I always wanted the Korean culture to be introduced to the world, and so I thought Taekwondo to be the most ideal item.

Lesniak: Okay.

Rhee: For Korean.

Lesniak: Sure, and how long did it take you to realize that dream? What age were you when you …?

Rhee: 10 years.

Lesniak: Only 10 ten years?

Rhee: Yes.

Lesniak: Okay, and you spent that time training, preparing, learning Taekwondo?

Rhee: That's right. I came 1950s, so probably it was 1956, to US.

Lesniak: Okay, and what did you … How did you start teaching Taekwondo when you arrived in the US?

Rhee: Well, first I learned … I just taught exactly the way I learned. Then I had a lot of new ideas. You know, some of the ideas they are teaching was very … too primitive, and so we have to be really improved. That's how I really started.

Lesniak: Okay. Great. Stories. I love stories. I told you before we started the recording that stories are kind of my favorite part of what we do here, and I'm sure that if I asked you to name them all, I mean, it would be books and books, and some of the stories that you've told are in books that I've read, but if I asked you to pick one of your favorite stories for our listeners, what might that be?

Rhee: Well, my new enlightened view of the world. This is my honest opinion. I was a devout Christian, and when I woke up with new ideas, Jesus Christ did not come just to create a little dinky church. He came here to build a Kingdom of Heaven and Earth. So, the philosophical term would be Utopia, so, I named the book called *Trutopia*. Have you heard of this book?

Lesniak: I have. I haven't had the chance to read it, but now that you're on the show, I'm going to.

Rhee: Do you have one?

Lesniak: I do not.

Rhee: Okay, when you finish, you can email me your address, email address … your mailing address, then I will send you one.

Lesniak: Oh, thank you, sir. So, tell us about this book then.

Rhee: Well, what this book is about, we made … You know, all the religions make dogma out of nonsense. It doesn't make sense. It's out of human reason. You know that, right?

Lesniak: Yes. Yes, I can relate.

Rhee: So, when they believe that, and they create a lot of, fabricate the stories, like Jesus Christ was born without father. I mean, that's very unnatural. That would never happen, and that Jesus' body went to Heaven. This is really fooling the ignorant people, but intelligent, educated people would not believe that, but they are afraid to say, "Oh, I don't believe that."

They said the perfect human being must appear, you know, like Jesus Christ, before we can start building Kingdom of Heaven and Earth. I decided maybe volunteer myself, and that I proclaimed that I am a perfect human being, in other words, divine human being means opposite of animal human being. Opposite … Animal human being always lie. Divine human being never lie.

Lesniak: Yeah.

Rhee: So, I made sure to practice for last 30, 40 years to be honest.

Lesniak: You talked about dogma within religion, and dogma within martial arts is a subject that comes up fairly frequently, and not just on this show, but in conversations martial artists have in the do jang. Do you see parallels there, and what do you think of that?

Rhee: No. No, Jesus Christ hate religion. He thinks that religions are making this world so crazy. You agree with me on that?

Lesniak: Yeah.

Rhee: And so, he is not religious person. He is a philosopher. Human being, just like you and I.

Lesniak: Right.

Rhee: After he died, the Bible came out, truth came about 300 years later, and they can fabricate any way they want.

Lesniak: Yes.

Rhee: There was no Jesus talk back to them.

Lesniak: And I've heard some people, and I'm curious of how you feel about this with Taekwondo, because you were around in the early days. Do you …?

Rhee: Yeah, Taekwondo … See, a lot of people didn't think of Taekwondo as philosophy. I wasn't either. How can punching and kicking people be philosophy? Well, first of all, our first responsibility to God is protecting the safety of our life, so we are responsible to learn how to defend under evil circumstances. We have to … Never fail … In other words, the world became crazy. Right?

Lesniak: Right.

Rhee: You agree?

Lesniak: Yes.

Rhee: Why? Why is it so crazy? Because people lying. You know? Let's say … Trump. Trump would lie to Soviet Union. Soviet Union lie to US. So these lies keep going, and later on, it's very hard to trust, so they try to build the most dangerous atom weapon they can find. That's atomic and hydrogen bomb. What a dangerous place to live here.

Lesniak: Right. Right.

Rhee: Especially when we have like people Kim Jong-il. You know?

Lesniak: Okay. You've talked about truth, honesty …

Rhee: Yes.

Lesniak: … a few times, and you've said that it's something that you've spent quite a few years working to hone, to make sure that you are honest.

Rhee: Okay, now let me ask you to repeat after me.

Lesniak: Please. Sure.

Rhee: When I am truthful …

Lesniak: When I am truthful …

Rhee: … my heart is beautiful.

Lesniak: … my heart is beautiful.

Rhee: When my heart is beautiful …

Lesniak: When my heart is beautiful …

Rhee: … everybody loves me.

Lesniak: … everybody loves me.

Rhee: When everybody loves me …

Lesniak: When everybody loves me …

Rhee: … I am happy.

Lesniak: … I am happy.

Rhee: Isn't that simple?

Lesniak: It is simple, and that is good logic.

Rhee: Mhmm. Oh yeah, it's very plain logic. And so, we never knew why we were living. The purpose of life was not clearly taught to the people. What do you think it is?

Lesniak: I've always thought it was to be happy.

Rhee: That's right.

Lesniak: Okay.

Rhee: Our purpose of life is to be happy. Yeah, you have to happy. In order to be happy, you have to be loved. See, Jesus Christ, all the religious leaders say, "You better live and die in my honor." That's the way introduced, you know, to scare people, but God never asked us to honor for him. He always say, "Forget about me. Just love one another." Even physical parents, never asked parents, "You better be honoring for me." You know what I mean?

Lesniak: Mhmm.

Rhee: How can a God ... He is not egomaniac.

Lesniak: Okay.

Rhee: Am I making sense?

Lesniak: You are, and I'm curious what - because these are good principles, these are good lessons - what do these look like ... Because I'm assuming at some point you took this into your teaching.

Rhee: Yeah.

Lesniak: Into the way you taught Taekwondo.

Rhee: Mhmm.

Lesniak: So, how did your Taekwondo teaching change as you brought these principles in?

Rhee: It did not change. Well, I introduced seven physical qualities of a champion.

Lesniak: Okay.

Rhee: Yeah. In order to be champion in Taekwondo, you have to have power, speed, timing, endurance, balance, flexibility, and good posture. There are seven corresponding, seven qualities of a human champion, identical. That's why, now, I said it's a philosophy. A very in-depth philosophy I found. Can you see?

Lesniak: Yeah. You …

Rhee: So in the power place, knowledge. Speedy place, you have to do the things quickly. You have to read a lot of books to be able to think very fast; and punctuality, timing; and persistent, perseverance; flexibility, you have to be flexible with your heart, just like your body is; and you have to have good balance, your body, mind, and heart. Body, mind, and heart, it must be balanced. In other words, strength in the body, honest in the heart, knowledge in the mind. So when you have your everything balanced, when you have all that, you are literally divine human being. You see?

Lesniak: I do.

Rhee: Mhmm.

Lesniak: I do.

Rhee: You never lie, you love people, then we are divine. We must, you know, think, "We are able to do anything we want to." I think when I first came to US, inventing new musical form and safety gear, I could not believe I did it. As you grow and build your confidence, anything you can do it.

Lesniak: If you were to take all of this knowledge that you have now and these understandings, and go back to when you were 24 or 26, and you had come to the US, and you started teaching, what would be different? Would there be less focus on physical things?

Rhee: Would be, of course. All would be the same, but totally different.

Lesniak: Okay.

Rhee: Yeah. Maybe I may have several thousand divine human beings now. And once it is a formula that works, it will be done within 21st century, because when we start in Washington, doesn't mean we have to finish Washington, and then next go to Moscow. It spread simultaneous time, all over the world. So maybe in a few decades, every country will have divine human beings.

Lesniak: Do you think a martial arts practice is part of that journey?

Rhee: Yes.

Lesniak: Okay.

Rhee: Yes.

Lesniak: Because of what you spoke of before with the need to defend, the protection element, or is it more than that?

Rhee: Well, more than one meaning, "protect my body."

Lesniak: Okay. Alright. More than just the literal interpretation of protection then?

Rhee: That's right.

Lesniak: Okay.

Rhee: We're not supposed to war. Right now, we are having a difficult fight, and that becomes expanded to become national fight, and world fight.

Lesniak: Yeah. What do we, as all martial artists today, if we think of martial arts as Taekwondo, and Karate, and Judo, and all martial arts, what do we as martial artists do wrong? What one thing would you want us to change?

Rhee: We aren't doing anything wrong. We're doing what everybody else is doing. We are trying to be good from normal evil. So, never lie, always love people. God will say, "I love you." "I hate Him. God, I hate you." "I still love you." We have to be in that position. Not easy.

Lesniak: No. Certainly not.

Rhee: That's why Jesus said, "Love thy enemy." You know, when He was baptized in the Jordan River by John the Baptist, the first thing He said is, "Repent, for the Kingdom of Heaven is at hand." He thought now He was baptized He was ready, but He didn't know. He is not all-knowing. Let me tell you, let me prove that to you.

Lesniak: Okay.

Rhee: When Romans tried to arrest Him, He was not trying to hide. Judah kind of sold the information for 30 silver, and that's how He was caught. Right?

Lesniak: Yeah.

Rhee: If he was all-knowing, why didn't he make helicopter and run away?

Lesniak: It's true.

Rhee: Simple question. Simple question. So when they start lied, their lie has to become bigger and bigger and justify that.

Lesniak: Yeah. Okay. If we could live in some kind of alternate world, where Jesus was doing martial arts, how do you think He would have approached His training?

Rhee: I think He would have do it exactly the way I did.

Lesniak: Really? Okay.

Rhee: Mhmm.

Lesniak: How so? Tell us more.

Rhee: Well, teach the seven qualities of a champion, so you become, you know, a perfect human being. Then, you can manage your family, your village, your city, your country.

Lesniak: Okay.

Rhee: There should be no disease, pain. All diseases were created from our own stress.

Lesniak: I would agree. I have heard people break down the word disease into dis-ease, to say you are uneasy, and that creates it. Other than Jesus, was there anyone that you would have wanted to train with that you didn't get to?

Rhee: Well, you know I trained with 350 US members of Congress, right? You've heard of that?

Lesniak: I did know that, yes.

Rhee: Oh. Naturally, I like to teach, I like to work out with those who have influence around him. That's why I picked Jesus, and then the US Congress.

Lesniak: Okay.

Rhee: They promote better than you and I can together.

Lesniak: Okay. Who was your favorite teacher?

Rhee: Mr. Uhm Woon-kyu in Korea.

Lesniak: Okay, and why him? Why was he your favorite?

Rhee: Because he was very talented in Taekwondo, and very easy to explain, to understand. Some people are gifted.

Lesniak: As teachers, you mean?

Rhee: Yeah.

Lesniak: What do you think makes a good teacher?

Rhee: I think enthusiasm, for first. He really, really have a will to teach, then. Anybody can be a good teacher.

Lesniak: It's not every day I get to speak with someone who has done as much to promote martial arts as Grandmaster Rhee. It's been a few days since we recorded, and I'm finding myself reflecting on the time often. It was a personal victory to have him on the show, and for him to be so open with me was certainly an honor. Thank you, Grandmaster Rhee, for coming on the show.

You can find us on social media - Facebook, Twitter Pinterest, YouTube, and Instagram - and our username is Whistlekick. You should also check out our Facebook group, Whistlekick Martial Arts Radio Behind the Scenes. Hit up our Amazon Book Store for an unabridged version of our Superfoot Bill Wallace interview. We have some other books over there, too, and even more in the works.

Thanks for listening to this episode, and hopefully you'll check out others.

Until next time, train hard, smile, and have a great day.

We Want to Hear from You!

Reviews are an important part of how others find our books, and they help us create content you love. If you enjoyed this book, please visit the associated Amazon product listing and leave us a review. We will use your feedback to help create more content catered towards you, our loyal readers.

Thank you!!

DON'T MISS OUR EVENTS!

ALL-IN WEEKEND

This 2-day martial arts event will be half training experience and half retreat. The cost of the event includes all of your training, your lodging, food, and an event shirt. All you have to do is show up, and we'll take care of the rest.

FREE TRAINING DAY

whistlekick's Free Training Day is exactly what the name says - one day of the year where martial artists come together to share and learn, all for free. There is no admission fee at this event, instructors are not paid, and whistlekick picks up the tab for the venue and any other logistical costs.

MARTIAL SUMMIT

Martial Summit is our vision for the future. A place where martial artists, from all over the world, of all systems and styles, come together to share. This 4-day event includes Free Training Day Northeast as well as the Never Settle Awards Banquet.

Follow the QR codes above or visit whistlekick.com and click on "For Individuals" to find all the latest info on our incredible events!

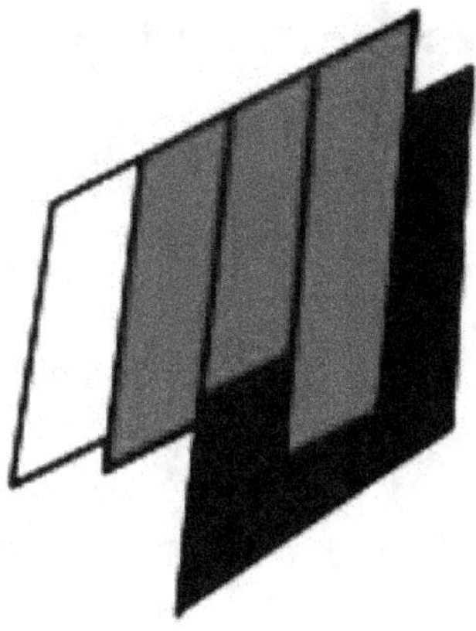

MartialJournal.com is a collective of passionate martial artists from all backgrounds, styles, and walks of life. We write because we enjoy sharing our knowledge and opinions and hope that you enjoy reading what we share.

Check us out!

Available from whistlekick Books

By Jenni Siu

The Origin of Master Hopkick Series

Book One: Beginnings
Also available in Special Edition
Book Two: Lessons
Book Three: **COMING SOON!**

By Jeremy Lesniak

Fiction

Faith: A Story of Unlikely Heroes in a Grim World
(The Katana Chronicles Book 1)
Book Two **COMING SOON!**

Non-Fiction

The Martial Artist's Handbook
12 Months to Health
How Not to Hold a Martial Arts Tournament: Practical Advice –
and Cautions – When Holding Martial Arts Competitions,
Seminars or Other Events
AND MORE!

Search us on Amazon for more titles!

wK Books

12 Months to Health

This book is designed to help you establish and reinforce 12 simple, inexpensive habits to achieve a healthier you in 12 months.

Visit us in our Facebook group for more:
https://www.facebook.com/groups/12mth

"Mr. Lesniak has laid out a well-researched, simple, and gradual guide to real success in incorporating healthy habits into one's daily life. I look forward to sharing this with my patients as a partner in their journey toward better health."

— Joshua Singer, Licensed Acupuncturist at River Street Wellness, Montpelier, Vermont

"Setting just the right goal is hard to do, and starting with consistent, bite-sized, achievable goals is the way to achieve real change in your health."

— Irvin Eisenberg, Masters in Occupational Therapy, Structural Integrator and Owner of Resilience Occupational Therapy

"Our healthcare system, as it is built, right now, is largely not designed to help you until AFTER chronic disease strikes. Even preventative health endorsed by your doctor is left to the small choices you make daily, by yourself, well outside of the walls of the clinic."

— Joshua T. White, MD, MBA, Chief Medical Officer, Gifford Medical Center

"12 things that ANYONE can do that will make a vast difference to their life."

— Daniel Eagles

"A single focus for a month makes it much more likely that I will be able to make sustainable changes."

— StaciAnne KaeLeigh Grove

FREE whistlekick Flexibility Program!

Yes, I said FREE! This program is designed by and for martial artists with features you won't find in any other program, at any price. The Flexibility Program is rooted in the latest science, immensely effective, and different from what most of us were taught.

The FREE whistlekick 30-Day Challenge

The program is a FREE and COMPLETE standalone training program you can start at any time. It's designed to be done on its own, without other strength or conditioning programs. The daily workouts can be completed in about 10 minutes, require NO EQUIPMENT, and can be done in a small indoor space.

This program combines martial arts and fitness to get you the exact workout you need on that day. It helps you build momentum to gain more out of your time – with your health, fitness, training, and the rest of your life.

These are just a sample of the programs we offer!

Looking to increase your speed? How about your fighting endurance? Visit whistlekick.com to see how we are revolutionizing the way you train to improve not only your martial arts skills, but also your overall health.

Check out the collection of whistlekick Programs in the whistlekick Store today!

We Truly Appreciate You!

Thank you for supporting whistlekick Books. As a member of the whistlekick family, we invite you to visit us at whistlekick.com. While there, you will find links to check out our other books, our events, our store, social media, how to leave us reviews, info on our other projects, and much more.

We are always open to your thoughts, questions, and suggestions. You may contact us anytime at books@whistlekick.com.

Thank you!

wK Books

Want to Find More?

This book was based on the one-on-one interviews with legendary guests featured on whistlekick Martial Arts Radio. You may find these episodes and more at whistlekickmartialartsradio.com.

You may wish to check out one of our other titles, including *The Martial Artist's Handbook*, an introduction to topics related to practicing martial arts for fans and practitioners alike. Find the library of whistlekick books on Amazon by searching "whistlekick books".

www.ingramcontent.com/pod-product-compliance
Lightning Source LLC
Chambersburg PA
CBHW071617150726
48000CB00004B/1765